Why L.A. Happened
Implications of the
'92 Los Angeles Rebellion

Also by Haki R. Madhubuti:

Poetry
> *Think Black*
> *Black Pride*
> *Don't Cry, Scream*
> *We Walk the Way of the New World*
> *Directionscore: Selected and New Poems*
> *Book of Life*
> *Earthquakes and Sunrise Missions*
> *Killing Memory, Seeking Ancestors*

Criticism
> *Dynamite Voices: Black Poets of the 1960s*

Anthologies
> *Why L.A. Happened: Implications of the '92 Los Angeles Rebellion*
> *Say That the River Turns: The Impact of Gwendolyn Brooks*
> *To Gwen, With Love* (co-edited with Pat Brown and Francis Ward)
> *Confusion By Any Other Name: Essays Exploring the Negative Impact of the Blackman's Guide to Understanding the Blackwoman*

Essays
> *Enemies: The Clash of Races*
> *From Plan to Planet, Life Studies: The Need for Black Minds and Institutions*
> *A Capsule Course in Black Poetry Writing* (co-authored with Gwendolyn Brooks, Keorapetse Kgositsile and Dudley Randall)
> *Black Men: Obsolete, Single, Dangerous? Afrikan American Families in Transition*

Why L.A. Happened
Implications of the
'92 Los Angeles Rebellion

Edited by Haki R. Madhubuti

Third World Press . Chicago

First Edition
First Printing 1993

ISBN: 0-88378-094-1

Manufactured in the United States of America.

Third World Press
7822 South Dobson Street
Chicago, IL 60619

Cover art: *Shango Loves L.A.* by Ammar
Cover design by Cheryl Catlin

DEDICATION

To the families who lost loved ones in L.A. 1992—
the fires in their hearts are still burning.

ACKNOWLEDGEMENTS

This book could not have been completed without the work and careful eye of Donna Williams, senior editor at Third World Press. We also would like to give a thousand thanks to all of the writers/artists who responded and contributed their works.

H.R.M.

CONTENTS

part three: MEDIA: NO MELODY OR ANALYSIS

part seven: **MORE TO REMEMBER**

INTRODUCTION

Same Song, Different Rhythm

It is not accurate or, for these times, bold enough to just say that America has a race problem. Without doubt or hesitation, I would say that America *is* a race problem. This is not new knowledge. This is not hidden revelation or numbed voices crying to the choir. America was founded and cut its trails on the blood of the indigenous people (First Nation People) of this land, viewing to this day Black folk (people of African descent) as step children to be moved at will on its chess board of the "New World Order."

The fires in Los Angeles are still burning. However, there are few fire trucks that can quiet these flames. These fires are in the hearts and minds of the people who believed, really believed, that America would be different, would be fair, just and good—yes, believed that America would return their love. Fire has a way of getting one's attention, James Baldwin warned us a generation ago. Malcolm X, in his unique manner, instructed us that America does not respect or listen to former "slaves" who follow the "rules." It is in the "rules" observation that Black folk are caught in a double bind. As the saying goes,

Why L.A. Happened

"damned if you do, damned if you don't." African Americans have tried the moral high ground, the moral middle, and now we are back to scorched earth.

Welcome to L.A. 1992.

This book exists because, like many of you, I am tired of hearing voices outside of our community telling us what the *problem* is or what *time* it is. I'm in Chicago, and on our block, the burning of L.A. after the Rodney King brutality verdict was not unexpected. In fact, one of the reasons why Chicago did not go the way of L.A. was because there was serious discussion and a healthy venting of anger. And anger—raw and unhollywoodish—is what we are talking about. Anger for unfulfilled promises, anger toward legislators who backstepped on policies decided, passed and not implemented, anger pouring undiluted toward a rulership that feeds on greed and exploitation and views Black people as enemies or as necessary burdens to be thrown crumbs like animals in their latest theme park.

All over the United States, there are people who live in obscene riches and obscene poverty within blocks of each other. There is a middle class, but for those—Black, white and other—who live in the economic center, there is a realization that there are few signs of it growing. A generation after the so-called "civil rights" revolution the larger question remains, Does America work for or care about the growing majority who are not white? The answer is a resounding *NO!* The L.A. insurrection—a going to the streets of the unheard—was another warning shot across the lawn, through the middle of the golf course, right outside the oval office of the White House.

Many of the rulership who are in a country club brain warp blame the '60s for the revolt in Los Angeles. However, for us, any independent activity that questions the rights of the few to literally shit on the lives of the growing disenfranchised is a hopeful sign. Quality leadership in the United States is extremely difficult to develop in the current political climate where its takes tens of millions of dollars to be elected a U.S. senator. The failure of political leadership has been monumental and has left unmarked graves across the landscape. Politics is a game played by professionals, paid for by businesses and special interests and believed in by the people. This is supposed to be what Democracy is about?

People who have money have a major voice and are able to buy many votes. If one is not white, regardless of how talented or gifted he or she is, the chances of him/her functioning at his/her zenith is highly doubtful. We live in the age of Desert Storm, BCCI, Savings & Loans theft, Irangate and countless other deals that the average citizen knows nothing about. Contrary to misinformed beliefs, America is not about fairness, decency, honesty, fair dealism or the rewarding of those who work. America is about being a part of the Club, about who you know and to what degree one is willing to compromise integrity and values, i.e., getting elected at any cost—the Willie Horton guarantee.

The violence in L.A. was a wake-up call from urban America. It was not just a Black hello but a Black-led multicultural notice where Latino, white and Asian peoples let their voices and fists be heard. L.A. was a call from the streets where Uzis and 9 millimeters spoke a different language to the empowered. Promises, unfulfilled from Watts, Detroit, Newark, Chicago, will not be replayed in the '90s. MTV and *Terminator 2* have given the under-30 a new reality. Rap and hip hop are not urban phenomena but are musical translations from Harlem to Miami. White House press conferences do not reach the listeners of Public Enemy, Sister Souljah, Queen Latifah or Ice-T.

The question is not always, Who is right? but, Who will be heard? Will the message of concerned activists ultimately translate its life-giving and life-saving solutions? There is a very large segment of this society who does not apologize for the '60s but looks upon that time as the decade that changed

Why L.A. Happened

America for the best. The '60s volcanic motion produced a significant number of men and women—of all backgrounds and races—who will *never* settle for the easy answers or compromises and have, against great odds, decided to be cultural/political activists for life. They are the writers, teachers, scholars, poets, artists, musicians and cultural workers who did not see L.A. as a riot but as a full-scale rebellion against obscene privilege and unspeakable corruption. That within the L.A. rebellion were people who looted, killed and took advantage of the crisis must not be understated or condoned. However, we feel that there are other stories that are not being told.

Most of the contributors to this book are, in their own way, long-time liberation fighters. We offer a more significant and in-tune analysis that hopefully brings some reasoned balance to the media beating of the *L.A. Times*, *Newsweek*, *Time*, CNN, the *Washington Post*, the *Wall Street Journal*, the *New York Times*, *Commentary* and the major networks. Our voices were not called upon by whitestream media to analyze the uprising in L.A. We are the "community" experts who, because of racism, class and sex biases, are overlooked; when published or aired, our voices are dismissed because they are not white or connected.

The cowardly and unlawful beating of Rodney King was not an aberration but follows a trend stemming from the Civil War. Black people's rights are stampeded upon in America, making the Constitution with its Bill of Rights, for a significant number of people, just words on a piece of faded paper. The major factor separating Rodney King from J.T., Big Willie or any other young man of color was a videotape shot by a concerned white man who did not allow his color and privileged status to stop him from doing the honorable thing.

Real political and cultural struggle is about the building of a world where men and women can act honorably and not feel that they have betrayed the "race," the brother/sisterhood, the clan or the party when they act in a way that does not conform to police state practices. Yet, a part of the problem is that "the leadership" is so treacherous.

In my lifetime, there have been only a handful of men and women on the national landscape in leadership positions who have not been bought off, sold or remade in the image of roaches crawling the floor with palms up.

Why L.A. Happened is our answer to business as usual. The women and men represented between these covers view the L.A. insurrection as a national and international crisis and therefore feel that it is our duty to voice opposition to faulty analysis and blatant racism that violates individual rights. Our participation is not only to pen urgent and eloquent responses, but we understand that part of the proceeds from this book will go into the Third World Press Prison Literature Fund. In 1991, TWP donated more than 10,000 books to inmates across the country.

It is clear to some of us that George Bush's New World Order is closely akin to Aldous Huxley's *Brave New World*. The major distinction is that *this is not fiction*. The Reagan and Bush revolution has neutralized many powerful movement voices of the past. Their silence has more to do with the availability of fewer and fewer outlets to voice opposition. *Why L.A. Happened* is our answer to the Daryl Gateses, Dan Quayles, Pat Buchanans, William Bennetts and other protectors of evil and injustice.

This will not be our final word.

Haki R. Madhubuti
Chicago
August 1992

part one . . .

WE ARE MORE THAN JUST HERE

Riot
Gwendolyn Brooks

A Poem in Three Parts

> *A riot is the language of the unheard.*
> —Martin Luther King, Jr.

John Cabot, out of Wilma, once a Wycliffe,
all whitebluerose below his golden hair,
wrapped richly in right linen and right wool,
almost forgot his Jaguar and Lake Bluff;
almost forgot Grandtully (which is The
Best Thing That Ever Happened To Scotch); almost
forgot the sculpture at the Richard Gray
and Distelheim; the kidney pie at Maxim's,
the Grenadine de Beouf at Maison Henri.

Because the "Negroes" were coming down the street.

Because the Poor were sweaty and unpretty
(not like Two Dainty Negroes in Winnetka)
and they were coming toward him in rough ranks.
In seas. In windsweep. They were black and loud.
And not detainable. And not discreet.

Gross. Gross. "Que tu es grossier!" John Cabot
itched instantly beneath the nourished white
that told his story of glory to the World.
"Don't let It touch me! the blackness! Lord!" he
whispered to any handy angel in the sky.

But, in a thrilling announcement, on It drove
and breathed on him: and touched him. In that breath
the fume of pig foot, chitterling and cheap chili,
malign, mocked John. And, in terrific touch, old
averted doubt jerked forward decently,
cried "Cabot! John! You are a desperate man,
and the desperate die expensively today."

John Cabot went down in the smoke and fire
and broken glass and blood, and he cried "Lord!
Forgive these nigguhs that know not what they do."

THE THIRD SERMON ON THE WARPLAND

Phoenix:
"In Egyptian mythology,
a bird which lived for five hundred
years and then consumed itself in fire,
rising renewed from the ashes."
—Webster

The earth is a beautiful place.
Watermirrors and things to be reflected.
Goldenrod across the little lagoon.

Why L.A. Happened

The Black Philosopher says
"Our chains are in the keep of the keeper
in a labeled cabinet
on the second shelf by the cookies,
sonatas, the arabesques...
There's a rattle, sometimes.
You do not hear it who mind only
cookies and crunch them.

You do not hear the remarkable music—'A
Death Song For You Before You Die.'
If you could hear it
you would make music too.
The blackblues."

West Madison Street
In "Jessie's Kitchen"
nobody's eating Jessie's Perfect Food.
Crazy flowers
cry up across the sky, spreading
and hissing **This is
it.**

The young men run.
They will not steal Bing Crosby but will steal
Melvin Van Peebles who made Lillie
a thing of Zampoughi a thing of red wiggles and trebles
(and I know there are twenty wire stalks sticking out
of her head
as her underfed haunches jerk jazz.)

A clean riot is not one in which little rioters
long-stomped, long-straddled, BEANLESS

but knowing no Why
go steal in hell
a radio, sit to hear James Brown
and Mingus, Young-Holt, Coleman, John,
    on V.O.N.
and sun themselves in Sin.

However, what
is going on
is going on.

Fire.

That is their way of lighting candles in the darkness.
A White Philosopher said
"It is better to light one candle than curse the darkness."
    These candles curse—
inverting the deeps of the darkness.

GUARD HERE, GUNS LOADED.

The young men run.
The children in ritual chatter
scatter upon
their Own and old geography.

The Law comes sirening across the town.

A woman is dead.
Motherwoman.
She lies among the boxes
(that held the haughty hat, the Polish sausages)
in newish, thorough, firm virginity

Why L.A. Happened

as rich as fudge is if you've had five pieces.
Not again shall she
partake of steak
on Christmas mornings, nor of nighttime
chicken and wine at Val Gray Ward's
nor say
of Mr. Beetley, Exit Jones, Junk Smith
nor neat New-baby Williams (man-to-many)
"He treat me right."

That was a gut gal.

"We'll do an us!" yells Yancey, a twittering twelve.
"Instead of your deathintheafternoon,
kill 'em, bull!
kill 'em, bull!"

The Black Philosopher blares
"I tell you, **exhaustive** black integrity
would assure a blackless America.... "

Nine die, Sun-Times will tell
and will tell too
in small black-bordered oblongs **"Rumor? check it
at 744-4111."**

A Poem to Peanut.
"Coooooool!" purrs Peanut. Peanut is
Richard—a Ranger and a gentleman.
A Signature. A Herald. And a Span.
This Peanut will not let his men explode.
And Rico will not.
Neither will Sengali.

Nor Bop nor Jeff, Geronimo nor Lover.
These merely peer and purr,
and pass the Passion over.
The Disciples stir
and thousandfold confer
with ranging Rangermen;
mutual in their "Yeah!—
this AIN'T all upinheah!"

"But WHY do These People offend **themselves?**" say they
who say also "It's time.
It's time to help
These People."

Lies are told and legends made.
Phoenix rises unafraid.

The Black Philosopher will remember:
"There they came to life and exulted,
the hurt mute.
Then it was over.

The dust, as they say, settled."

GWENDOLYN BROOKS, the first Black to win a Pulitzer Prize, is a graduate of Chicago's Wilson Junior College and has been awarded more than 60 honorary degrees.   She has published 16 books including poetry, children's verse, writing manuals, one novel and an autobiography.   In 1985 she became the 29th appointment as Consultant in Poetry to the Library of Congress. Ms. Brooks holds the Gwendolyn Brooks Chair in Black Literature and Creative Writing at Chicago State University.

From Slavery to Rodney King:
Continuity and Change

Tony Martin

Some of us become at times drunk with our power
and authority, and, in the fullness of our narrow
conceit, wreak our vengeance upon others under the
guise of justice. Oh, how wanton is man!

—Marcus Garvey

There is no justice but strength...Might is right, and
if you must be heard and respected you have to
accumulate...those resources that will compel unjust man to think twice before he acts.

—Marcus Garvey

In a sense little has changed. We came here in chains.
News photos of persons arrested during the Los Angeles riots
were sadly and maddeningly evocative of slavery. Hundreds of
men and women lay face down on the street, hands tied behind
their backs, while policemen walked among them (and probably on them, as seen in the live, real cops and robbers shows
now popular on TV). Here were the slave coffles of old, the
slave ships with hundreds of human beings trussed like animals
and packed like sardines. On the five hundredth anniversary of
Columbus, the man who started it all, little has changed.

Why L.A. Happened

Slavery meant poverty. Black people are still inordinately represented among the poor. Slavery meant confinement to the slave quarters. Many Black folk are now confined to wretched living conditions in segregated environments. Slavery meant the wanton killing and maiming of Black people. The Rodney King brutality case and a host of other recent cases from around the country, say the same. Even when the atrocities are captured on film—Latasha Harlins shot in the back of the head by a Korean woman, Rodney King beaten almost to death for no good reason—the message remains the same. The Supreme Court in the Dred Scott case of 1857 held that Black people have no rights that white people are bound to respect. The Simi Valley jury affirmed that decision. The Thirteenth Amendment to the Constitution in 1865 abolished slavery except as a punishment for crime. Incarcerated persons are therefore slaves, which doubtless explains why the United States has the highest imprisonment rate of any nation in the world and why 85% of Black men in Washington, DC can expect to be arrested during their lifetimes. Slavery lives.

It was during slavery that the notion of Black folk as animals took root among white people. Black people were not only bought, sold, hunted, corralled and brutalized like animals. The race was further subjected to the intellectual rationalization of such actions. Thomas Jefferson, in his *Notes on the State of Virginia* (1783), argued that Africans required less sleep, felt less grief, were less intellectually endowed, had stronger sexual urges and stank more than 'regular' human beings. Furthermore, he asserted African women preferred sex with orangutans over intercourse with humans. (Jefferson is said to have had five children with Black Sally Hemings, which presumably makes him somewhat of an orangutan himself.) The Simi Valley jury appears to have bought the argument that King grunted like an animal while being beaten, which struck fear into the hearts of his heavily armed assailants and justified their near-homicide. Beating him nearly to death thus became a humanitarian gesture, since the only alternative to subduing the animal would have been to shoot him.

From the Reconstruction period of the late 19th century to the early decades of the 20th, African Americans were lynched almost on a daily basis. Black men, women and children were hung from trees and lamp posts, burned on woodpiles in public places and shot to pieces before frenzied mobs sometimes numbering into the thousands. Ears, noses, lips, fingers, toes and genital organs were cut from the corpses as souvenirs. Sometimes the white crowds literally fought over these grisly remains. A white crowd once joined hands and sang "Happy Days Are Here Again" around a mutilated corpse.

The perpetrators would often profile smilingly around the charred remains. The resulting photographs would be made into postcards and sent through the mails. The usual verdict for these acts of public murder in the few cases that resulted in an inquest was "death by persons unknown." Government officials were "powerless to intervene," to paraphrase the words of Governor Theodore G. Bilbo of Mississippi in 1919. Bilbo was here commenting on a newspaper headline, "3,000 Will Lynch Negro Tomorrow."

A lynching took place in Los Angeles. For Rodney King, the video camera replaced the still photographs of old. The perpetrators were equally well identified. The verdict was the same. The powers that be were "powerless" to do justice, rendered temporarily impotent in the face of injustice to an African person. As in the case of the murder of young Emmett Till near Money, Mississippi in 1955, a white (or mostly white) jury refused to convict white men for lynching a Black person.

Racial riots have a long and unfortunate history in this country. Until fairly recently, most riots consisted of white mobs attacking and killing Black people. In the New York Draft Riots of 1863, white crowds roamed the streets killing and brutalizing any Black people they could find. In East St. Louis in 1917, whites set fire to the local Black neighborhood and killed Black folk as they fled the flames. It is only in recent decades that Black people have taken the initiative and always in response to some racial provocation. The police have been the cause of more Black-initiated riots than any other factor. The Houston Riot of 1917 began when white policemen manhandled a Black woman and brutalized the Black soldier who came to her aid. The Chicago Riot of 1919 began when a white policeman refused to apprehend white persons who had stoned a Black boy to death as he swam in Lake Michigan. The Watts Riot of 1965 in Los Angeles was triggered by the excessive force used in arresting a Black man for alleged drunk driving. The Detroit Riot of 1967 started as a reaction to police brutality accompanying the arrest of 70 to 80 African-American patrons of a speakeasy. The "Rodney King" Riots of 1992 were no different. They were caused by blatant police brutality compounded by an incomprehensible verdict on the side of bigotry.

Many races and nations who have come into contact with white supremacy over the last 500 years have disappeared from the face of the earth. The Caribs and Arawaks of the Caribbean are no more. The native peoples of North America, like the Amerindians of Central and South America, have been savagely decimated. Eight to twelve million Africans died in the so-called Belgian Congo in the last two decades of the 19th century. The Kohi-San people of South Africa were largely exterminated. The surviving remnant of the Aborigines of Australia are in a situation similar to the native peoples of North America. The original Tasmanians are no more.

Africans were first brought to the Americas because of their perceived ability to withstand the rigors of the most oppressive regime known to human history. The Spanish priest who was largely responsible for their importation, Bartolome de Las Casas, thought that one African could do the work of four so-called Indians. He thought that Africans could never die (or so it was alleged). The Africans, in fact, died like flies, which caused Las Casas to repent for encouraging African enslavement. But it was too late. Unlike the Amerindians, however, the Africans survived. They have continued to survive. Here and there they have even prospered.

Crucial to the survival of Africans in this hostile environment have been two factors—fearless leadership and unrelenting struggle. These factors will have to be wedded to economic and political power before freedom, justice and equality are achieved. But they have been sufficient to ensure survival, no mean feat in the circumstances. Despite enforced illiteracy during slavery and enforced inferior education thereafter, African Americans have managed to maintain a sense of historical continuity in a struggle that has defied the most aggressive advances of bigotry and hate.

Much of that struggle has been mobilized through the power of organization. Contrary to popular belief, there probably is no other community in these United States more adept at organizing than African Americans. Whether in the church or on the streets, in academia or Congress, the African-American flair for organization is beautiful to behold. The Montgomery Improvement Association was put together in the metaphorical minute, and the rest is history. Marcus Garvey arrived penniless in the United States in 1916, and by 1919, his Universal Negro Improvement Association was the most powerful Pan-African movement of all time. Denmark Vesey organized thousands of slaves for miles around Charleston for an entire year before being betrayed on the eve of striking in 1822. Many are the unsung and unknown persons who have organized "spontaneous" demonstrations, protests, boycotts and the like in reaction to a thousand injustices over the years.

And always, at the root of organization, has been the willingness in the final analysis to make any sacrifices necessary. Whether it was Malcolm X speaking out in the face of imminent death, or young members of the Black Panther Party in 1966 patrolling the police, or the enraged citizens of Los Angeles unleashing awesome righteous power in 1992, the

31

reality has been clear. The African-American population, when pushed to the wall, has always been a force to be reckoned with. "Let your motto be resistance!" said Henry Highland Garnet in 1843. "Power concedes nothing without a struggle," said Frederick Douglass, "it never did and it never will."

Ethnic groups that have made it into the American Dream have traditionally stepped on the necks of African-American communities on their way up. Jews, Italians, Greeks, Chinese, Arabs and now East Indians and Koreans have all, to greater or lesser degrees, quickly assimilated this Fundamental Law of Immigrant Upward Mobility. Black folks in Harlem had to picket Jewish stores in the 1930s and 1940s with signs saying "Don't Buy Where You Can't Work." Black people in Brooklyn, New York in the 1990s had to boycott Korean businessmen accused of assaulting a Black female customer. In each case the powers that be decreed the boycotts and pickets illegal. In Los Angeles not long before the Rodney King outrage, a female Korean shopowner shot the teenaged African-American girl, Latasha Harlins, in the back of the head at point blank range. This, too, was captured on videotape and shown around the world. For this act, even more cold-blooded than the King beating, the Korean woman was sentenced by a white female judge to a suspended sentence and a few months probation.

The actual or potential bigotry of many of these immigrant groups has been encouraged by the powers that be in an effort to find buffers against African-American advancement. The Korean problem in African-American Los Angeles, highlighted during the so-called Rodney King riots, is the newest manifestation of an old phenomenon. Now, as before, thousands of African Americans have to purchase their daily needs from Ethnic Americans who take their money, sometimes ensconced behind bullet proof barriers, while treating their Black customers with hatred and contempt.

The riots of the 1960s, the Civil Rights movement that preceded them and the Black Power movement that accompanied them, paved the way for Black elected officials. Black mayors are now much more commonplace than they were two or three decades ago. Stokely Carmichael (now Kwame Toure) once warned that "Black visibility is not Black Power," though it may be added that it is at least a step along the way. The Rodney King episode provides an opportunity to reflect on the limits of Black political power at the present time. Clearly the mere presence of a Black mayor in Los Angeles was not sufficient to prevent or even punish gross police abuse. In Philadelphia, not many years ago, we witnessed the spectacle of a Black mayor presiding over the aerial police bombing of a Black neighborhood in his own city—something which has happened only once before in North American history, namely during the Tulsa riots of 1921. Tulsa was a straight case of racist whites attacking Black people. Philadelphia and Los Angeles are far more complex. Are they arguments against African-American political empowerment? Of course not. But they painfully demonstrate the limits of such power at the present time, while economic power and federal, state and much of city political power remain in white hands. In the wake of the Rodney King affair, Los Angeles has hired itself a new African-American police chief. Black folk can wait and watch and pray that this individual may do the right thing. Blind hope based on pigment alone will, however, be misplaced.

In Los Angeles it may be agreed that a Black mayor electorally dependent on a significant portion of the white community finds himself in a racial straightjacket. In Atlanta, however, the aftermath of the Simi Valley verdict brought the brutal invasion of a Black college campus by a much more racially entrenched Black administration. This Black administration was willing to resort to repressive measures to prevent its Black students from demonstrating their anger over the verdict.

In the national media, as in politics, African Americans have made progress since the 1960s. The media equivalents of

Why L.A. Happened

Black mayors are, however, still to appear. Even more than in the realm of politics, Black media visibility has not yet achieved Black media power. Black newscasters, weather reporters and talk show hosts are not often the arbiters of news perspectives.

Never was the need for African-centered analysis more painful than on national television during the period of the L.A. riots. The major public and private networks ran an endless and nauseating stream of commentary by white people who appeared not to have left their ivory towers for some time. They also exercised great ingenuity in finding Black people to denounce the riots.

Their favorite argument was that the responsible and respectable middle-class African-American community was totally hostile to the anger being vented by their underclass brethren and sistren. "Yes, the verdict was unjust," they kept saying, "but hoodlums have taken advantage of the situation to riot." While the media excoriated the angry Black community, they glorified the armed whites and Koreans preparing to kill presumed looters. Koreans were shown in the streets firing weapons, movie style, at persons unknown and unshown, and presumably Black. While Blacks and Hispanics were blamed for most of the rioting, little information was forthcoming on the racial composition of the enormous casualty toll. It remained for the Black press to suggest that a large number of the dead were victims of police bullets.

No event since the death of Malcolm X and Martin Luther King, Jr. has so affected and enraged African-American opinion across class lines as the Simi Valley decision. To suggest that the African-American middle class was overwhelmingly out of sympathy with those who gave tangible expression to their anger was to resort to a hostile contrivance.

The authentic Black voice appeared only infrequently amidst the barrage of panel discussions, commentaries, news reports, speeches and talk shows. ABC's *Nightline* was, wittingly or unwittingly, responsible for more than its share. There

34

was Congresswoman Maxine Waters, representative of the rioting district, a figure of great honesty and resolve, even in the midst of great anguish. There was the Reverend Jesse Jackson saying that even he, a Black man, could not walk the streets free from fear. And there was host Ted Koppel's attempt to pit two gang members against the pastor of a community African Methodist Episcopal church. The attempt backfired embarrassingly in Koppel's face as the preacher forcefully declared his solidarity with gang members and everybody else. In the midst of this debacle Koppel, perhaps unintentionally, allowed a national television audience a rare opportunity to hear the authentic voice of Los Angeles gang members. It was a sophisticated voice and probably engendered discomfort in some quarters. It was a voice which placed the immediate situation in the context of hundreds of years of unrelenting oppression of the African American, from slavery to the present. It was a voice which was very aware of the FBI's Counter Intelligence Program (COINTELPRO) of the 1960s against the Black Movement. One gang member made the interesting point that some of Los Angeles' notorious "drive by" shootings are actually the work of law enforcement agencies applying COINTELPRO-style tactics to pit groups of Black people against one another. The gang members, finally, used the occasion to promise reconciliation among rival gangs and a united front against police excesses.

What happened in Los Angeles—the police brutality, the unjust verdict, the angry response—are part of an ancient spiral. The spiral will continue in the absence of fundamental change. Any fundamental long-term change will have to result in power, political and economic, for the African-American community. Without power there will be no solution, without strength there will be no justice, and without justice there will be no peace.

Events in Eastern Europe and Southern Africa have shown that change can come dramatically and violently where injustice and ineptness have been allowed to fester. Black America today comprises a sophisticated and conscious population with emerging leaders of great ability. A quiet revolution has taken place whereby for the first time ever, Black folk can now discuss and dialogue among themselves, from publisher to author to distributor to bookseller to audience, without total dependence on non-Black enterprises at any critical step along the way. The African-American masses are reading, perhaps more so than the middle classes. The level of sophistication and historical knowledge shown by gang members on the *Nightline* program is indicative of this. Yet, even as the African-American middle class has made some gains, and even as the truly rich (athletes and entertainers in particular) have made some spectacular advances, the masses have become more impoverished, and institutional racism has remained entrenched.

The need for Black self-reliance as a way out is now widely acknowledged. Black conservatives have belatedly rediscovered the concept. The Black nationalist community has striven for self-reliance since time immemorial. Even the integrationist community, traditionally reliant on white philanthropic assistance, seeks "independence" from such support. Booker T. Washington moved the race several steps forward on the principle of self-reliance one hundred years age. Marcus Garvey built the most successful mass movement in our history around the same principle. Elijah Muhammad and the Nation of Islam demonstrated the great possibilities of self-reliance.

But self-reliance in the African-American community has historically been frustrated by the most obstinate forces of bigoted law and custom. Self-reliance is made doubly difficult in the face of denial of equal access to mortgage monies and business loans, by differential access to basic municipal services, by limited access to proper education, by governmental repression of the advocates of self-reliance and by the legion of institutionalized injustices that beset the community.

Yet, the community has to find some way to build

economic power while negotiating these overwhelming hurdles. As Booker T. Washington might have said, the removal of these fetters on Black progress will redound to the benefit of the entire society. At a time when North America can no longer expect automatic pre-eminence in the world, it may not be in the majority's interest to squander the creativity and talent of 12% of its population. The Black creativity and talent that have exploded through the openings made in sports and entertainment are set to explode again as the walls of prejudice are breached in new areas, such as education, entrepreneurship and science. Perhaps it is fear of this pent-up ability that helps fuel the intransigence of continued racism.

Black folk have to continue the struggle against these barriers. It is too late for the forces of reaction to turn this struggle around now. If an irresistible force of Black struggle were to meet an immovable object of entrenched bigotry, the results could be cataclysmic. Marcus Garvey feared that such an eventuality was likely and would end in disaster for an outnumbered African-American population. Hence his desire to see an alternative and countervailing base of Black power in Africa.

Leon Trotsky saw a disaffected African-American population taking advantage of a foreign invasion of the United States to secede. In the 1960s and '70s, the Topographical Research Centers in Chicago and elsewhere agreed that the way to avoid annihilation was for Black folk to regroup, as it were, in the South. Some day a disenthralled and united Caribbean may provide safe haven and support for an African-American revolution thereby fulfilling the promise of the Haitian Revolution.

In the past, the irresistible force of African-American struggle has ebbed and flowed, strategically retreating after periods of intense battle in order to rest and recuperate. The immovable object of bigotry has moved just enough to avoid cataclysm when Armageddon seemed possible. Whether the painfully slow progress implied in this process will continue to satisfy either side remains to be seen. Dramatic change for the better or even more explosive turmoil are as likely as continuing slow change in the face of fierce resistance.

There are many lessons to be learned from Rodney King. For some, the lesson may be that control of the Black plantation needs to be strengthened. After the riots of the 1960s, it is said, highways were built through and around Black communities, making them easily isolated in times of unrest. Some police departments adopted the feared dum dum bullets, outlawed in international warfare but legal in domestic law enforcement. Buildings erected in Black communities often resembled fortresses, all brick and nary a glimpse of glass. For some, the lesson may be that these measures have not been effective. More draconian measures may be devised. Final solutions may be proposed.

For others, the lesson may be that the system needs to retreat some more. African Americans, after two hundred years of the Constitution, should finally be allowed a jury of their peers. The police should be overseen by civilian review boards. A predominantly white police force should not patrol a predominantly Black area like a force of alien occupation. Maybe some enterprising politician will coin a catchy phrase like "Great Society" or "New Deal," and hope will spring eternal once more.

For the thinking person, the lesson should be that despite its creativity and skill, despite its awesome constructive and destructive power, African America still remains entangled in the constraining web of institutionalized bigotry. Redressing specific wrongs is necessary, but not sufficient. The problem presses down in so many directions that proposed long-term solutions can easily degenerate into platitudes.

Perhaps the unfolding revolution in African-centered book publishing, and similar developments in audio-visual products and in film, may provide a base of consciousness to fuel the educational, economic and political thrust that is now unavoidable. Indications are that the very wealthy of the race may often be disposed to invest their money in socially conscious ways. But whether they are or not, they can still be induced to invest in the race if presented with proposals that are as profitable as those to be found any place else. There is an opportunity here for financial creativity on the part of those who understand the system under which we are forced to live. If too few of us understand that system, then maybe the time has come for some of us to study it. African-American creativity let loose in the world of finance and entrepreneurship may yet replicate the gains made in entertainment and sports.

Other races and groups in the North American melting pot/salad bowl have amassed resources in various ways. Not a few have used organized crime to seed money into respectable enterprise. Most have cornered some segment of the economic or political marketplace—garment trades, labor unions in this or that industry, skilled trades, police departments, the restaurant business, the film industry and so on. Now that Black folk have begun to reap some benefits from their hitherto unrewarded athletic and entertainment skills, perhaps an opportunity may be at hand.

The basic humanitarian instincts of Black folks and their unfortunate historical experience as the victims of world capitalism have profoundly shaped African-American attitudes to the accumulation of financial resources. Yet, with the apparent collapse of world socialism and the undistinguished racial record of North American socialists, alternative strategies are few. Booker T. Washington, Marcus Garvey and Elijah Muhammad all grappled with this question. They all tried, in differing ways and with some success, to stress the accumulation of group wealth while not falling prey to the stupidity of modern day Black conservatives who preach self-reliance while maintaining a safe distance from their African-American community. For all his apparent conservatism, Booker T.

Why L.A. Happened

Washington was rooted in African-American life in a way that modern day Black conservatives are not.

The immediate day-to-day struggle for survival in African America is intense and can be all-consuming. Yet, out of that daily response to a thousand indignities must come the vision of long-range salvation. The community has risen to many challenges in the past, and it must now rise to the challenge for concentrated thought and positive action. Let justice be done to Rodney King. But let him also be a catalyst for the long term.

DR. TONY MARTIN is professor of Africana Studies at Wellesley College. A leading scholar of the Marcus Garvey movement, he has authored several books including *Marcus Garvey, Hero: A First Biography* (1983); *The Pan-African Connection* (1983); and *Race First: The Ideological and Organizational Struggles of Marcus Garvey and the Universal Negro Improvement Association* (1976). Dr. Martin has also edited: *Literary Garveyism: Garvey, Black Arts and the Harlem Renaissance* (1983) and *The Poetical Works of Marcus Garvey* (1983).

Rodney King and Dred Scott

Alphonso Pinkney

> Our eyes did not deceive us. We saw what we saw
> and what we saw was a crime...The jury's verdict
> will never blind us to what we saw on that videotape.
> —Mayor Tom Bradley of Los Angeles

April 29, 1992 was a significant day in the long struggle of Black people in the United States, for it was on this day that the words of Chief Justice Roger B. Taney of the Supreme Court in *Dred Scott v. Stanford* (1857) were reaffirmed by a jury in Simi Valley, California. Speaking for the court, Chief Justice Taney said that Blacks "were so far inferior that they had no rights which the white man was bound to respect." In essence that is what the Simi Valley jury told the world when they acquitted four white police officers of assaulting Rodney King, a Black man, in the early morning hours of March 3, 1991.

The facts in this case (*California v. Powell*) are not in dispute because the incident was viewed repeatedly on television throughout the world, thanks to George Holliday who videotaped this barbarous act and to Cable News Network that broadcast it.

What the videotape showed the world was the prostrate body of a hog-tied Rodney King being savagely beaten by four

Why L.A. Happened

police officers while 19 others looked on approvingly. Altogether he was clubbed 56 times in just 81 seconds. His injuries included nine skull fractures, a shattered eye socket, a broken leg, a fractured cheek bone, a concussion, nerve injuries that left part of his face paralyzed and burns from a Taser electric stun gun. During the beating, one policeman, who delivered 15 blows, could be heard laughing and making racial slurs. After the beating, King was thrown into an ambulance and driven to a hospital.

The four police officers were ultimately indicted by a grand jury, but the 19 who watched were not. The grand jury found no violation of California law, according to the District Attorney. He said, "However morally wrong their failure to intercede, in California there is no criminal statute under which these officers can be indicted." He called their behavior "irresponsible and offensive." Under California law, it is not possible to prosecute police officers for such serious crimes as aiding and abetting, accessory after the fact or dereliction of duty in failing to stop a crime.

The beating administered by the police officers was so egregious that it was condemned around the world. In addition to Mayor Tom Bradley, President George Bush, not known for his support of civil rights, condemned the jury's unconscionable verdict. In a televised news conference he said,

> Yesterday's verdict in the Los Angeles police case has left us all with a deep sense of personal frustration and anguish...What you saw and what I saw in the TV video was revolting. I felt anger. I felt pain. I thought, how can I explain this to my grandchildren?

Daryl F. Gates, the Los Angeles police chief long known for his contempt for people of color, wrote in his book *Chief: My Life in the LAPD*:

> I stared at the screen in disbelief. I played the one-minute fifty-second tape again. Then again and again, until I had

viewed it twenty-five times. And still I could not believe what I was looking at. To see my officers engaged in what appeared to be excessive use of force, possibly criminally excessive, to see them beat a man with their batons *fifty-six times*, to see a sergeant on the scene who did nothing to seize control, was something I never dreamed I would witness.

He continued, "It was a very, very extreme use of force...I sat there watching, terribly shocked. Feeling sick to my stomach, sick at heart."

The *New York Times* editorialized that "the King verdict brutalized faith in law, and in law enforcement...Far from discouraging uncontrolled police brutality, the trial jury's action seemed to *validate* it." Elsewhere in the world the condemnation was severe. The Libyan government newspaper *el-Fajr-al-Jadid* wrote: "There is no guarantee of justice in the American legal system for the rights of those with non-white skin." And the official Libyan news agency, JANA, asked: "How can a state where justice is unbalanced and human rights are not respected raise the banner of defending human rights in the world?" *Peoples Daily*, the newspaper of the Chinese Communist Party, said, "Facts show that U.S. society is not at all what has been proclaimed by America's human rights apologists. Ruthless facts shattered this peaceful picture they painted."

The Los Angeles police chief said the incident should be considered an aberration rather than a pattern of racial bias. However, the audio tape of police communications released after the beating shows that although the officers knew the injuries to King were serious, they joked with each other and with the desk officer shortly after the beating. In transcripts of the communications among police cars the supervising officer at the scene reported: "You just had a big time use of force." The officer at the communications desk replied, "I'm sure the lizard didn't deserve it. Ha, ha." These comments among the officers were so casual that they lend support to frequent reports that Los Angeles police officers routinely engage in acts of brutality against Blacks and Hispanics.

In the Constitution of the United States, both Article III and the Sixth Amendment address criminal trials, but neither deals specifically with change of venue, except to say that such trials must be held in the state where the crime(s) occurred. However, the Constitution does guarantee defendants the right to a fair and impartial jury. For example, if a defendant believes that he/she will not receive a fair trial because of local pre-trial publicity, a request can be made for a change of venue to another location.

Such a request was made for this reason by defense lawyers in the case of the four police officers charged in the beating of Rodney King. The California Second District Court of Appeal granted a change of venue on July 23, 1991 because of the extraordinary publicity generated by the videotaped beating of King. Judge Stanley M. Weisberg of Superior Court moved the trial from Los Angeles 35 miles away to largely white Simi Valley in suburban Ventura County, a conservative city of 100,000 people, some 2,000 of whom are Los Angeles police officers and retirees. Simi Valley is a city whose residents "worship the police," according to a law professor, and one that is politically, racially and culturally as different from downtown Los Angeles "as Manhattan is from the moon," said a lawyer.

Compare the demographics of Los Angeles and Ventura Counties. According to the 1990 census, Los Angeles county is 57% white (including white Hispanics), 11% Black and 21% people of other races (including non-white Hispanics). Ventura County, on the other hand, is 80% white (including white Hispanics), 2% Black, 5% Asian and 13% people of other races (including non-white Hispanics).

The demographic characteristics of the jurors involved in this miscarriage of justice present an interesting picture. Of the

264 potential jurors, the six who were Black were excluded from service by peremptory challenges, i.e., no reason had to be given for their exclusion. Seven males and five females were finally selected. They were largely blue-collar workers: a painter, a grounds worker, a telephone installer, a cable splicer, a hospital housekeeper, a computer programmer and a nurse. Five were retired, and the average age was 51 years. Five were registered in the Republican party and five in the Democratic party. Three were members of the (conservative) National Rifle Association, and three were relatives of police officers.

The racism of the Simi Valley jurors was equalled only by their contempt for justice and the facts in the case. In an interview after the verdict, one of the jurors told a television reporter that she had voted to acquit the police officers because (an unarmed) Rodney King had repeatedly resisted arrest and "was in full control of the situation," although 23 (armed) officers were present. Another juror criticized the quality of the videotape and questioned the seriousness of King's injuries. "A lot of those blows, when you watched them in slow motion, were not connecting," she said. "Those batons are heavy, but when you looked at King's body three days after the incident, not that much damage was done." And the forewoman of the jury reported to the court that the acquittals were decided during the first day of deliberations. The deliberations were indeed a farce because the jurors had decided to acquit the officers before proceedings had begun.

It is clear, then, that the site for the trial and the composition of the jury ordained the verdict. The residents of Simi Valley were just as likely as those of Los Angeles to have viewed the beating, since it had been shown repeatedly throughout the world. Furthermore, it is naive to assume that in the United States, a society obsessed with race, that a near all-white jury would reach conclusions similar to one with Black members.

A few days after the verdict, Judge W. Thomas Spencer

of the Dade County Florida Circuit Court, recognizing the importance of diversity in jury trials, especially those dealing with racial issues, changed the venue of a trial of a white police officer charged in the deaths of two Black men in Miami in 1989.

After the trial in Miami in which the policeman was convicted by a multi-ethnic jury, an appeals court ordered a retrial, ruling that the jurors probably feared that an acquittal would have triggered riots. Judge Spencer moved the trial from Miami to Orlando in Orange County, but after the Simi Valley verdict, he announced that the trial would be moved from Orlando to Tallahassee. He said he had done so because only 10% of potential jurors in Orlando were Black, while in Tallahassee, 21% were Black, as was the case in Miami.

In announcing the new change of venue, Judge Spencer said: "This court cannot ignore the national tragedy of the urban riots occurring after the Rodney King verdict. That so many of our fellow Americans feel shut out of our judicial system demands our attention." He continued, "This court is convinced that, rightly or wrongly, Orlando is now perceived as not providing the necessary framework for an impartial trial." In this regard, Judge Spencer demonstrated greater awareness of the racism in the American criminal justice system and a greater sense of fairness than did Judge Weisberg.

In the American criminal justice system, venue is often determined by political considerations. During the Vietnam war, for example, the government of the United States frequently decided to have its infamous conspiracy cases tried in favorable (usually conservative) locations. This is illustrated by the trial of the Harrisburg Seven in 1972. In this case, J. Edgar Hoover of the Federal Bureau of Investigation encouraged the Department of Justice to indict seven anti-war activists (largely Catholic priests, nuns and students known as the East Coast Conspiracy to Save Lives) on three counts: conspiring to raid draft boards, conspiring to kidnap presidential advisor

Henry Kissinger and conspiring to blow up heating tunnels in Washington, DC.

The activities of these anti-war activists were well publicized. The indictment specifically mentioned draft board raids in New York, Philadelphia, Rochester and "other parts of the United States." The Justice Department selected the middle district of Pennsylvania. Within this district the government had a choice of Harrisburg, Lewisburg or Scranton. Lewisburg is a college town, and college students tended to be liberal, especially in opposition to the Vietnam war. Scranton contained a high proportion of Catholics, Democrats and sometimes militant mine workers. Harrisburg, on the other hand, had a majority of Republicans in its population, few Catholics, a high proportion of fundamentalist religious groups, several military installations and war industries and an active Ku Klux Klan. It was the belief of the prosecutors that they were more likely to get a favorable verdict (conviction) in Harrisburg than in Lewisburg or Scranton.

The case can be made that Judge Weisberg selected Simi Valley for the same political reasons that the Justice Department selected Harrisburg. The appeals court directed simply that the case be moved from Los Angeles. Why not a multi-ethnic location like Berkeley, Oakland or San Francisco? Judge Weisberg maintained that Simi Valley was selected because of convenience and cost, but these are hardly more important considerations than fairness and justice. Or are they? When justice for Blacks is involved, the answer is obvious.

In the United States only the accused may appeal a perverse verdict on the grounds that it cannot be supported by the evidence presented. Constitutional guarantees against double jeopardy preclude such action in an acquittal. While this is an important protection for the accused, it led to a miscarriage of justice in the Rodney King brutality case.

The jury in Simi Valley was the functional equivalent of the Supreme Court in the Dred Scott case. Although their cases were separated by nearly a century and a half, Rodney King, like Dred Scott, was denied justice because he too is Black in a racist society.

The Simi Valley verdict was yet another outrageous chapter in American history. It proved to the world that the American criminal justice system continues to maintain two standards: one for whites and one for Blacks.

DR. ALPHONSO PINKNEY is Professor Emeritus, Hunter College, The City University of New York. He is the author of several texts including—*Black Americans*; *The Committed: White Activists in the Civil Rights Movement*; *The American Way of Violence; Red, Black and Green: Black Nationalism in the United States;* and *The Myth of Black Progress*. *Howard Beach and Other Atrocities* will be released in 1993 by Third World Press.

The Los Angeles Rebellion:
Seizing the Historical Moment

Anderson Thompson

"We are at war!" warns Sister Souljah. In this last quarter of the 20th century (from Watts, 1965, to South Central Los Angeles, 1992), it has become apparent that the Black world is finally waking up to the cold reality that we are the victim-captives of a *full scale war!* Africa, her people, land and resources, is the target. We have no army. We have no weapons. We are one billion African civilians. Many of us do not know what's going on, and others refuse to believe that *somebody's trying to systematically eliminate the entire African race.*

The Los Angeles rebellion was fundamentally grounded in the ongoing worldwide African Liberation Movement. When the infamous Simi Valley verdict was announced, the Black *world* immediately responded. From Soweto to L.A., Africans chanted "no justice, no peace." In America, the awakened Black masses took to the streets, openly rebelling against white supremacy.

THE "NEGRO" QUESTION

By their mere presence, inner city youth, a standing army with fearsome fire power, pose a serious challenge to America's

49

white supremacy war machine. Strategically situated at the jugular of America's cities—their downtowns and shopping malls—young Black warriors of Los Angeles, accustomed to fighting and shooting each other, have now momentarily stopped and raised the question, "Who is the real enemy?"

The Rodney King situation exposed the inability of the urban strategist to solve white America's oldest problem—The Negro Question, i.e., the troublesome presence of the Negro in the midst of white society. President George Bush and the Pentagon have found no workable formula for "Negro proofing" American cities against Black slave uprisings in response to the unannounced declaration of war against the African community of America. Spontaneous rebellions, demonstrations, looting, fires and pitched battles will be with America for some time.

Frederick Douglass in 1863 had this to say: "...men sneer at it as the Nigger Question, endeavoring to degrade it by misspelling it...The term Negro is at this hour the most pregnant word in the English language. The destiny of the nation has the Negro for its pivot, and turns upon the question as to what shall be done with him...."

A LUTA CONTINUA!
(The struggle continues!)

Black people are the world's oldest revolutionaries, the world's oldest freedom fighters. We are part of the longest resistance movement on earth. We have been fighting foreign invaders for 4000 years and have been under siege for 3000. Our struggles against Asia and Europe are not new. Since the 21st century BC and earlier, the Euro-Asian nomads have been attacking, disrupting, dismantling and pillaging the African world, her great kingdoms and civilizations. Fundamental to the conflict, race and skin color are two of the most indelible factors in the lives of every Black man and woman on this earth.

The Los Angeles Rebellion:
Seizing the Historical Moment

They carry with them a worldwide connotation of the European victor and his African victim, the white master and his Black slave, the colonizer and the colonized.

We know that the western white supremacy system regard Africans as members of a despised and innately inferior race who must submit to the will of Europe. The lethal stigma of African inferiority lies at the heart of the struggle for freedom all over the world. The mark of African inferiority plagues the Black race, from Soweto to Cairo, Illinois, from Harlem to Watts. If we fail to find a solution for this mental and spiritual affliction in our own lifetime, we can expect a future destiny of 21st century-style slavery and colonialism for our children and our yet unborn.

THE CHALLENGE OF THE 21ST CENTURY

In the 20th and upcoming 21st centuries, the New Negro Question for the Euro-Asian is how to successfully capture the Black man's mind so that Europe and Asia may trade, operate and profit anywhere in the Black world without restriction. In the theater of psychological warfare, we must first, at all costs, win this mind war. Our most urgent task is to understand the white supremacy system—its history, structure and function, how it works, who constructed it, what maintains it and how to defeat it. As Mr. Neeley Fuller teaches us in *The United Compensatory Code*: "If you do not understand white supremacy (racism) what it is, and how it works—everything else that you understand will only confuse you...."

In 1992, after 500 years of African resistance and warfare against Europe and more than 3000 years of struggle against Asia, this phase of our struggle, the Los Angeles Rebellion 1992, comes during a rising tide of African consciousness. The ideas of Black power, African Nationalism and the quest for a United States of Africa have reached their peak in the minds of our people. We are beginning to understand the ramifications of the violent, inhumane and barbaric scattering and dispersal

51

of the African family to all parts of the world which made us beasts of burden for Asia and Europe. In the '90s, we have finally come full circle.

Wars in the past were fought using rocks, arrows, spears, bullets and bombs to seize and control territory. By defeating and destroying the adversary, nations expanded their empires thus acquiring enormous wealth in land, resources and people. Today, the strategic battlefield and territory for conquest is the *human mind* itself.

THE GLOBAL WHITE SUPREMACY SYSTEM

There is not a Black man, woman or child living on this earth today who has not been physically or mentally violated by the crippling effects of an all encompassing global system of white supremacy, the white man's ultra-modern war machine.

The term "white supremacy" best describes the system of warfare presently at work to conquer the world today. It is that system that makes war against all persons of African descent. It is a system of ideas and methods, based on the myth of the inherent superiority of the white race and the inherent inferiority of the Black race. It is the European drive for mastery and war against nature, God and society and the aggressive drive to rule the world that has brought the whole of humanity to where we are today.

The sickness and disease of white supremacy is embedded deeply in every sector of European culture and society and has infected and polluted the entire African world community. The menace of global white power remains elusive despite the universal exploitation and oppression of Black people everywhere in the world.

The African community of America has a special role to play as it enters the 21st century struggle of the three worlds of Africa, Europe and Asia. The struggle between Europe and Asia to conquer the world, with global Black people as the battlefield, is by far our greatest challenge.

The Los Angeles Rebellion:
Seizing the Historical Moment

The breakup and dismemberment of the Soviet Union drove home a hard lesson to the African Nationalist intellectual community. As far back as we can remember, the United States and Russia had been sworn enemies, engaged in super power standoffs, each packing enough nuclear weaponry to destroy planet earth and part of heaven. After four decades of nuclear feinting and millions of dead African freedom fighters on either side of the United States and Russia, we find the two in bed together. It is clear that white supremacy on the left is no different than white supremacy on the right. White is right even when it's left!

ASIAN SUPREMACY

Our trouble with Europe is a relatively recent four hundred year-old encounter. Africa has had an Asian problem for *thousands* of years. Black anger in Los Angeles has its roots in a 4000 year-old battle against a well-known adversary. In 2070 BC, surrounded on all sides by her Asiatic invaders swarming in from land and sea, an old African king passed on the following instructions to his son and successor, Pharaoh Merikare of the 9/10th Dynasty:

> Lo the miserable Asiatic, He is wretched because of the place he is in. Short of water, bare of wood, its paths are many and painful because of mountains. He does not dwell in one place. Food propels his legs, he fights since the time of Horus not conquering nor being conquered. He does not announce the day of combat, like a thief who darts about...Do not concern yourself with him. (Vol. 1, *Ancient Egyptian Literature*, ed. Miriam Licteim)

Lo! the miserable Asiatic of Los Angeles, selling wigs, hats, handbags, basketball/jogging shoes, automobiles, VCRs, TVs, radios and tape recorders! He has levied a full scale economic interpenetration of the entire African world. Like a parasite, he "attacks" the African consumer, boring from within, attaching himself to an already hapless and hopeless African victim tightly held in the vise-like grip of an already consuming predatory European economy.

Lo! the miserable Asiatic of Los Angeles, the frightened, heavily armed Korean business owner, the new urban cowboy firing at the alleged L.A. looters, armed with rifles and automatic weapons.

The western empire nations and her new Asian settlers are bleeding the African continent dry. Together each year they extract hundreds of billions of dollars worth of raw materials, resources and human labor, leaving our people to suffer from droughts, famine, disease, coup d'etats, high interest loans and newly arriving European and Asian settlers.

Which leads us to ask this question: Is there really a mad scheme afoot to exterminate the entire African race? Are Blacks in Africa and America facing genocide? Have we been targeted for elimination? AIDS spreads more rapidly through Black groups in Africa and America than any other. The telltale signs are evident. Remember the Indians who, misnamed to this very day, were hunted, tortured, debased and driven from their native lands in this country.

Similarly, Africans today are being driven from the lands. Crack, AK47's and Uzi's are being sold to our Black youth just like whiskey and repeater rifles were sold to the "Indians." Los Angeles is a modern day version of yesterday's violent removal and extermination of the "Indians" from their national homeland.

In the meantime, our Asiatic and Eastern European replacements have arrived. White yuppies (young, upwardly mobile professionals), their moms, dads and grandparents, are winding their way back to the centers of the city, joined by new waves of Koreans, East Indians, Vietnamese, Mid-east and Eastern Europeans. These new urban pioneers (along with their buppy (Black) imitators) are homesteading in the dangerous wildernesses of Black neighborhoods. If current trends continue, this resettlement in the inner cities will move Blacks to South African-styled Bantustans, miserable tribal townships of human labor located on the outskirts of each white city.

THE BLACK LEADERSHIP CRISIS

The seat of our salvation and survival as a people facing war and genocide is, without a doubt, our leadership. What is our grand vision of the future? What do we want for generations of unborn African children? Have we planned for the year 2092? Are we ready to struggle for a United States of Africa by the year 2020? August 2020 will mark the centennial of the UNIA International Conference during which 25,000 Africans, under the leadership of Marcus Garvey, unfurled red, black and green banners and declared Africa for the Africans. "I know no national boundary where Black people are concerned," wrote Marcus Garvey in the 1920s. "The whole world is my province until Africa is free...The ends that we serve are not of self but for the higher development of the entire race. I have a vision of the future, and I see before us a picture of a redeemed Africa."

The rich ideological legacy of our Black leadership in America has been the tension between influential Black men and women over which path best leads to freedom for the Black masses in America. Should the Black majority pursue as an end multiracialism and first class citizenship in America? Should Black people in America accept the western values of Black inferiority and accommodate segregation—an apartheid white supremacy system that dictates we stay in our place? Or should we seek, along with our white comrades, the destruction of capitalism and replace it with socialism or communism? Or better yet, should we elect to separate from white America and build an independent Black nation here, in the Caribbean or on the African continent?

The crisis facing our national Black establishment leaders in America is the race war against the Black world. Frighten-ingly, they have no response to the Euro-Asian scramble for

Why L.A. Happened

African minds which reaps: confiscation of lands, reshaping Blacks into 20th century slaves, extracting raw materials from poverty-stricken Black countries with the use of indigenous labor and selling the finished product back to a false Black middle class and its poor Black masses.

In fact Los Angeles, a microcosm of the struggle of the three worlds, shows that no city in the world is safe from its former slaves, colonies and exploited workers. Each colonial and slave capital of the world (Madrid, Paris, London, Moscow, Beijing, Baghdad, Mecca) is a potential tinderbox of revolution over the struggle between Europe and Asia for Africa. The empire builders of yesterday are in confrontation with today's generations of the oppressed. The offspring of yesterday's African victims have returned to haunt Europe's "new world order" and her new Asian imperialist cohorts.

THE AFRICAN PRINCIPLE

The African Principle—*doing that which is best for the greatest number of Africans living in the world today*—should be our guide for action. The African Principle equips and guides each African with a vision of the world, a sense of direction, a path leading to his/her future place in the world beyond his/her own personal pursuit of success and security.

There will be no justice, freedom or economic well-being for the millions of grassroot Africans in America unless our local and national leaders become uncompromising defenders of the African Principle, or those uncompromising defenders of the African Principle struggle to become our local and national leaders.

In its present form, Black electoral politics denies the African Principle and ignores the primary task of nation-building. The legacy of Black leadership in America has been a following of the European Principle while violating, compromising or sacrificing the African Principle for short-term, limited "Black strategies."

If, in the 21st century, our Black leaders and thinkers should fail us by overlooking our most obvious threat—the Euro-Asian control of the African mind—once again they will have broken the African Principle and exposed Mother Africa to another millennium of Euro-Asiatic servitude, exploitation and racial annihilation.

DEVELOPING THE
AFRICAN COMMUNITY OF AMERICA

First, we must begin the difficult task of developing a strong Nationalist/Pan-Africanist leadership in America. Enough of Black leaders cavorting with whites.

Our Pan-Africanist and Nationalist organizations—Nation of Islam, Universal Negro Improvement Association Party, Republic of New Africa, National Coalition of Blacks for Reparations in America, African Heritage Studies Association and the New National African Peoples Organization—find themselves in the dangerous position of lacking a consensus as to a future direction. However, Los Angeles can very well serve as a springboard for dialogue between the Nationalist/Pan-Africanist communities of America, addressing such issues as: *nationality* (what is the proper nationality for the 40,000,000 Africans inside America?); the *Pan-African unification* of the African world community; the *formation of local African communities* in each city, town and village; and *the organization of one strong collective community.*

Our most urgent task is to close ranks and make a decisive drive to win the hearts and minds of the Black masses in America. We must practice "...the essential selfishness of survival..." as our wise elder, John Henrik Clarke, instructs in his *Notes for an African-American World Revolution.*

The time has come to let our integrationist-assimilationist brothers and sisters go their own way, with our blessings. As Harold Cruse says in *The Crisis of the Negro Intellectual*, "It is a tactical error [for the nationalists] to waste their time, and energies and propaganda fighting and criticizing integrationists. The fallacies and weakness of integrationist programs can be exposed only to the degree that the nationalist initiate counter programs along political, economic and cultural lines...."

The following are some suggestions for committees, papers, task forces and commissions to help facilitate the union of the African communities of America:

1. A Declaration of Principles, Policies, Strategies and Practices for the African Communities of America
2. A council made up of representatives of the Nationalist/ Pan-Africanist organizations
3. A council made up of representatives from each city, town or village in America
4. A National Committee to Stop Genocide against Black People in America
5. A National Commission on Reparations and Repatriation
6. In response to the African-centered movement, an independent National Board of Education for persons of African ancestry
7. A National Student Network made up of Black students at the college and high school levels
8. A National Legal Defense Fund
9. A National Communications System
10. A National Committee on Sports and Entertainment
11. A National Committee for Economic Self-Reliance
12. An International Commission on Building African Universities
13. A National Board of Health
14. A National Fund for Scientific and Technological Research
15. A National Ministry of Defense

The Los Angeles Rebellion:
Seizing the Historical Moment

DR. ANDERSON THOMPSON is a professor of African and Middle-Eastern Affairs, Center for Inner City Studies, Northeastern Illinois University-Chicago. He is also Research Commissioner and a national board member of the Association for the Study of Classical African Civilizations.

How Do We Rage Safely?
Some Thoughts About Racism and the Psychological Consequences of Being Black in America

Vivian Verdell Gordon

To understand the mindset of those who abused Rodney King and who continue to abuse other African Americans requires that we depart from the *immediate* event and take a brief historic look at the nature of American racism. Such a review allows us to more clearly understand the full range of issues which go beyond Los Angeles to the psychological systems of definition and control that have crafted the present status of African people. Such a historical perspective will allow us to properly address immediate issues and develop a course of action.

On the emergence of American racism, Juan Gonzales writes:

> History books usually refer to the period of colonial expansion as the period of Exploration and Discovery. This, of course, refers to that historical period when European nations set out to claim and conquer new

61

territories. The primary objective was not only to obtain new territories for the mother country, but also to extract raw materials from these new lands and ship them home for processing and distribution...An additional advantage in their efforts to subdue the native populations, was the cooperation of the major religions who insured that the 'savages' were brought into the fold of Christianity and civilized. The fact that these indigenous groups were all 'People of Color' was of particular importance, as the Europeans were able to use the various racial theories, that were popular at the time, to justify the subjugation of racial groups throughout the world.

Important accompaniments to racism are sexism and economic exploitation. The "social order" wields its power (legal and illegal) against those outside the order. The dominant group establishes, enforces and interprets the rules that govern the order; superior attitudes and expressions of power manifest through these processes.

Sexism is enforced through physical dominance, which includes the potential for violence as well as rendering victims helpless and in need of protection. Accompanying institutionalized gender-based religious beliefs also promote the view of a divine order based on (white) male dominance/female subordination. All of this is skillfully reinforced through the use of sexual politics.

Economic oppression is the subjugation and exploitation of the "other" and is maintained through discrimination and seated in racism. Access to the rewards of the system is limited by those (white men) who control the means of production and distribution. Privilege and hierarchy based upon race and male gender ensures that others are blocked out. Local, state and federal military resources are often used to maintain control.

He who holds the power defines the truth. Racism, sexism and economic exploitation are all reinforced and justified through schools, media, religious institutions, etc. In schools, for example, historic accounts are continuously presented that defend the images of those in power. This contributes to a selective memory and perpetuates the racist theme.

In fact, in many schools today, children are still taught that there were good things that resulted from slavery, such as introducing Christianity to "pagan, savage people." They say that there were "good" masters who allowed the enslaved to rest on Sundays, the "bad" masters did not. Similarly, women are traditionally socialized to find a "good" man (an excellent provider) as opposed to a "bad" man (poor, broke). Thus, those who have access to the system of work and reward are "good," those who do not are "bad." Consequently, unemployment and underemployment are the fault of those who cannot find work. This, of course, becomes the foundation for white beliefs about Blacks. As reported by the *New York Times,* the Number One belief held by white Americans about Black Americans is that they are lazy and do not want to work.

THE CURRENT ISSUE

The extent to which power is victorious is important when considering its ability to control and define the social reality of the subordinate group. As others have written more powerfully than can I, power triumphs most when it controls the minds of the oppressed and promotes a victim's mentality. (Woodson, Fanon and others) Ultimate victory is achieved when those in power not only benefit from the moral and legal sanctions of the established systems but control the very definition of self and group worth of the victimized.

In their discussion about the struggle for identity and coping with oppression, two contemporary Black psychologists write:

> Long before the child can verbalize, he or she is aware of the fact that something is fundamentally wrong in the American society, that some pervasive, catastrophic,

and oppressive force is preventing African-American people from achieving their goals and participating in the range of opportunities that America provides for its citizens [Baldwin, 1963, referenced]. The complete impact of this awareness does not come all at once, but falls into place gradually during middle childhood, preadolescence, early adolescence, young adulthood, and later adulthood stages. As a child looks into the mirror image of society reflected in TV, movies, newspapers, and stories about the heroes of American history, he or she sees images of Euro-Americans projected with power, courage, competence, beauty and goodness. The conclusion that racism is pervasive in the American society has a profound, lasting, and often devastating influence on African-American young people. They may express their disappointment with anger, fear, resentment, or bitterness. This realization cannot help but generate a period of confusion in Black youth, because it forces them to have to deal with the contradictions that have been inherent in American society for over 350 years. (White and Parham)

Evidence of a victim's mentality abounds within the Black community. It ranges from the obvious fratricide (Black-on-Black violence) to the various forms of physical and psychological exploitation. Simply blaming racism, while at the same time participating in the destruction of self and community, represents the dis-ease of being Black in America. Difficult to diagnose and cure, this dis-ease manifests as the placid acceptance of inequality and exploitation on one hand, self-destructive rage on the other.

Without careful thought and correct directions, a new reality will be created—African people will be transformed into a predetermined negative mold; violence and destruction within the community and without will become a self-fulfilling prophecy. However, more important than the physical destruction of the community or the dangers facing and the stress of its residents, violence becomes an acceptable way of dealing with injustice and subordination. Not only will overwhelming numbers of people be incarcerated, moral fiber, based upon ancient African spirituality, will be lost. (Clarke, Hilliard, Karenga, Nobles, Van Sertima and others)

So, how do we rage safely? The answer begets yet another question: *What legacy do we wish to leave our children?*

This discussion is difficult given the pervasive sense of hopelessness and helplessness among African Americans. The current political and economic reality which, over the past 15 years has counteracted many of the limited gains achieved in the '50s and '60s, further impedes discussion. Consider, for example, the following complexities:

1. The average income of the Black male college graduate is equal to that of the white male *high school dropout.*
    (a) Theoretically, education allows people access to the system; however, inequality flourishes in the public schools. Today, as in the time of the Coleman Report, the education dollar follows the *white* child.
    (b) Theoretically, education is the primary way to access power; however, the cost of post-secondary education has increased while financial assistance has decreased. Additionally, some Black advisors advocate against race-specific financial assistance while ignoring the race-specific nature of the problem.
    (c) In the American educational system, cultural diversity is opposed by influential power groups who express "concern" about Black ethnocentricity while continuing to define civilization solely from a Greco-Roman perspective. That same group found no single Black work qualified for inclusion in *Great Books of the Western World.*
2. Labor advocates call for the retraining of both skilled and unskilled workers for the work of the "technological

future"; yet, employment opportunities are being reduced by the transport of business out of the country (to maximize profits).

3. Economic progress through a work program that will "rebuild the American infrastructure" is currently being touted; yet, Blacks continue to be locked out of skilled labor markets and apprenticeships required for senior licenses. Minority business set-asides continue to face legal challenges.

4. The environment concerns us all; but the daily litany of environmental racism continues to plague us (evidenced by the continued incidences of lead poisoning among young Black children).

5. Black people are encouraged to educate themselves about AIDS and other sexually transmitted diseases; but the memory of the Tuskegee syphillis experiment is still fresh. Furthermore, the medical establishment is seated in racism and sexism. Poor people often use emergency rooms as the family doctor because they lack adequate heath care insurance.

6. The youth are encouraged to invest in the future; yet, they consistently see the homeless and the destitute, which include disproportionate numbers of Black veterans. They see members of their community trapped in dead-end jobs in spite of their motivation and diligent work.

7. Young people are encouraged to delay gratification and plan for the future; yet, they see their seniors locked out of social security, medical insurance and pension plans.

8. Americans are assured that government will provide for the poor and the disadvantaged; yet, Blacks see that, within their own communities, those in need of public assistance usually benefit from only two government programs, compared to low-income whites who, on average, benefit from all seven of the major programs. (Hill)

9. Teen girls and boys are encouraged to delay parenthood

during a time in their lives when they are seeking to validate themselves in a society which denies them access. Consequently, for many young males, sexuality comes to mean "manhood"; for young females, motherhood provides the key to being a woman. The teens are further alienated by a system which defines manhood by one's ability to provide and protect (through economic resources) but denies opportunities for achievement. Correspondingly, the system perpetuates a sexism which equates feminine beauty with the Anglo-Saxon model and promotes sex as the way to "the good life." (To whom are our Black men singing about love, commitment and the good life on most of those BET videos?)

HOW DO WE RAGE SAFELY
TO BRING ABOUT CHANGE?

In addition to sanctioned social inequality and the State's power to control and define, the ultimate victory of racism is that the State controls *how* a people are allowed to rage. Mental health practitioners perceive those who respond to American racism with long-suffering as *sane*; those who respond with righteous indignation are diagnosed *insane*.

> The gravest danger we see is that unscrupulous people may use psychotherapy with blacks as a means of social control, to persuade the patient to be satisfied with his lot. Such would be a wicked abuse of the confidence of the unwitting patient as well as the confidence invested in professionals by the community. There will no doubt always be wicked persons capable of such things. The most important aspect of therapy with blacks, we are convinced, is that racist mistreatment must be echoed and underlined as a fact, an unfortunate fact, but a most important fact—a part of reality. Dissatisfaction with such mistreatment is to be expected and one's resentment should be of appropriate dimensions. It bears some

> resemblance to military psychiatry, where the psychia-
> trist must keep fit for duty the warrior whose primary
> function is to oppose the enemy. In America, the role of
> blacks, as for humans everywhere, is to live and flourish
> and to be fit progenitors of generations to come. To do
> so, they must oppose racism in an unrelenting way.
> Psychiatry for such warriors aims to keep them fit for the
> duty at hand and healthy enough to enjoy the victories
> that are certain to come. (Grier and Cobbs)

Unfortunately, one of the behavioral consequences of being Black in America is rampant self-destruction by angry people who participate in displacement or misdirected hostility. This misdirected anger threatens attempts to maintain an appropriate fitness for battle. Although it is a justified anger created from being told to endure and to trust in racist institutions, it is an anger which turns in upon itself to destroy. This anger holds many hostage in the Black community. To come to grips with it, we must clearly understand the extent to which power resulting from inequality allows the dominant to control and define the social reality for the subordinate. Pain is defined by those who cause you harm; they even tell you *if* and *when* you might cry.

Perhaps we should rage safely through the ballot. But should we vote for a Presidential candidate who, in a nomination acceptance speech, talked for a full 45 minutes—only a short time after the Los Angeles rebellion which resulted in the loss of 51 lives, 2,383 injuries and more than $785 million in damages—and *never once mentioned* racism in America? Should we vote for an incumbent President who walked quickly through the Black "riot" area and then convened a special meeting on the matter without inviting the area's Congressional representative to participate? A President who promoted the continued dismantling of programs designed to help South Central L.A. and other under-served communities while blaming conditions on those same late-coming and underfinanced programs?

Perhaps one rages safely by speaking out against inequality and the continuing patterns of racist behavior. But that could get you fired, or at best, passed over for select assignments and/or promotions. Most certainly, it will get you listed by the local police and other related authorities as a "potential troublemaker."

For example, Professor Derrick Bell, one of the country's leading legal scholars and author of *And We Are Not Saved*, found himself "fired" by Harvard University when, in protesting the university's failure to hire a Black woman as a faculty member, he went beyond a university two-year leave without pay policy. (One wonders how many Harvard faculty persons have been granted extended leave to serve as ambassadors and special advisors to government and private industry.)

When I served as the official spokesperson for Black faculty (at a historically white university) who were objecting to the extensive membership of school chairpersons and top administrators in a racist country club whose stated policy denied membership and even visitation to Blacks and Jews, I was told by one of my students, a police officer, that my name had been placed on the city's police list as a "potential troublemaker."

Should we return to the streets, picketing and boycotting? Should we define our own issues and select our own candidates? Should we promote massive voter registration and seize the political balance of power? Dare we call Black leadership into question? Dare we determine how our leaders will emerge and be defined? Should we support independent schools, and through our various religious structures, establish free Saturday schools for educational enhancement? Could the alumnae of historic Black colleges and universities change their focus from the homecoming game and the class reunion celebration to the appointment of the trustee boards and presidents?

Should we demand a change in media images by simply

turning our televisions off and not going to the movies or by refusing to buy the products sponsoring such programs? Should we demand anything less than quality films and positive images from Black filmmakers? Could we economize and not participate in conspicuous consumption, especially when merchants treat us poorly or do not offer us good services or when they "bell" for security as we move from department to department?

Should we promote literacy, assuming that a knowledgeable people will not allow anyone to tell them their truths? Could we not only wear symbolic dress, such as the kente of the Ashanti, but also purchase culturally relevant books so that we might both read and teach our children?

Ultimately, *even in the face of racism*, we must take control over our own lives. We must reclaim our cultural spirituality through an incorporation of the teachings of our ancient African ancestors into our contemporary daily lives. We must be willing to come together to listen, to learn, to study and to support each other. We must elect positive life styles which preclude the escapism of substance abuse and dependency. We must create a collective life style which places value upon diversity while maintaining community.

We can do it. We have no choice.

NOTES

1. Bulhan, Hussein Abdilahi. *Frantz Fanon and the Psychology of Opression.* New York: Plenum Press, 1985.
2. Gonzales, Juan L. *Racial and Ethnic Groups in America.* Dubuque, Iowa. Kendall/Hunt Publishing Company. 1990.
3. Cobbs, Price M., and William H. Grier. *Black Rage.* Introduction to the 1992 edition. New York: Basic Books, 1992.
4. Gordon, Vivian V. *Black Women, Feminism, Black Liberation: Which Way?* Chicago: Third World Press,

1989.

5.   Horseman, Reginald. *Race and Manifest Destiny: The Origins of American Racial Anglo-Saxonism.* Cambridge: Harvard University Press, 1981.

6.   Jones, Reginald L., Editor. *Black Psychology*, 3rd ed. Berkeley: Cobb and Henry Publishers, 1991.

7.   Nobles, Wade. *African Psychology.* San Francisco: The Black Family Institute, 1990.

8.   Parham, Thomas A., and Joseph L. White. *The Psychology of Blacks: An African-American Perspective.* Englewood Cliffs: Prentice Hall, 1990.

DR. VIVIAN VERDELL GORDON is a professor, Department of Africana Studies, State University of New York at Albany. She is a consultant on issues of race, ethnic and gender relations and cultural diversity. Dr. Gordon is the author of: *The Self-Concept of Black Americans*; *Lectures: Black Scholars On Black Issues*; and *Black Women, Feminism and Black Liberation: Which Way?*. She also co-authored *Think About Prisons and the Criminal Justice System* (for 5th grade to junior high).

part two . . .

HARD FACTS

Crossover Justice

Nathan Hare and Julia Hare

The uprising that occurred in Los Angeles after the Simi Valley verdict was more destructive than any hurricane (except Andrew) in the history of the United States. It presents us with an imponderable warning of the inherent injustice of jury proceedings based on the myth of a color-blind society. At the same time, it is a reflection of the overall obsolescence of the present day jury system spawned by the relentless decadence of a society that idolizes materialism; that is to say, property above people, possessions above character, technology and its devices above values.

Sociologists have called this the problem of the "cultural lag," where one section of culture (the nonmaterial or spiritual) lags behind in delayed development, while the material sphere of culture dominates. Unchecked and perpetually elongated, this tendency to worship technology and material development produces a situation in which society is extremely or overly developed technologically but neglected and stunted morally and socially. Its inhabitants are compelled to contend with the psychological condition of *anomie* (alienation and normlessness) in which old ways and expectations no longer are accepted or no longer apply. Its system of justice (putting race aside for a moment) will increasingly be dominated by technical gadgeteering—by omnipresent and quietly scanning video cameras looking down at us in banks and post offices, helicopters hovering overhead, their searchlights penetrating our bedrooms in the middle of the night, invisible radars and computerized scanners lurking along the freeway, our fingerprints and genetic matchups left behind as evidence for the prosecution. Surveillance fuses with the everyday environment, including random and anonymous citizens with video cameras on the streets or behind drawn curtains and window shades; news cameras in helicopters record street scenes from on high, as in the beating of Reginald Dennis, the white truck driver. But, with all of this, society will eventually gather to rest its case on an outmoded jury system that stubbornly and haughtily clings to obsolete manners such as may be most graphically portrayed by the British (and African males under their influence) donning snow-white wigs in courtroom proceedings dictated by doggedly ritualistic endeavors to follow archaic and catatonic juridical rules and regulations.

When it comes to race and social domination, the superodinate group's own machinery combines inevitably with a breakdown in its social apparatus to facilitate, if not to provoke, public disturbances against itself. This is but a microcosm of its more global tendency to self-destruct, now expressing itself in the ecological wreckage and pollution of the air and the atmosphere, of the ozone layer and the stratosphere, the destruction of its own species and the very earth.

Thus, while the similarities of the South Central Los Angeles uprising and the race riots of history are rigorously apparent, the difference is that previous disturbances were often sparked by some rumor, generally a spurious one. (In Tulsa of 1921, a Black male who stepped on a young white female's toe in a downtown elevator was said to have "attacked" her.) South Central LA, on the other hand, was kicked off by the stark credibility of a videotape shown on television night after night after night, backed up by daily front-page accounts and editorials and cartoons and columns condemning the centuries-old brutality Black people have suffered at the hands of white policemen and calling attention to the "devilish" history of the LAPD. And as we watched the many confrontations between paramilitary-minded Chief Gates and Black Mayor Bradley, we remembered:

PAMELA LOVE, the attractive, young woman who was shot down by policemen;

RON SETTLES, the California State-Long Beach football star found hanged to death in a cell in 1981;

OLIVER BEASLEY, member of the Nation of Islam, who was slain in 1990 by Los Angeles County Sheriff's deputies;

LATASHA HARLIN, the teenager who was killed by the Korean grocer in 1991—

—right on down to the beating of Rodney King.

Any discussion of this case must include an analysis of the change of venue to a courtroom in suburban Simi Valley—our hopes in the hands of a jury of ten whites, one Asian and one Hispanic, *no Blacks*.

Webster's *New World Dictionary* describes a change of venue as "the substitution of another place of trial, as when the jury or court is likely to be prejudiced." In the course of ensuring a "fair and impartial" trial, as provided by the Sixth Amendment to the U.S. Constitution, a change of venue represents a recognition of the limits of the efficacy of ordinary courtroom techniques of jury selection. However, it fails to recognize that there may be *no* venue in America where a Black person, particularly a young adult Black male, can obtain a fair and impartial trial.

Thus, while effecting a change of geography, change of venue ignores genotype (race of kind) and niche (returning to Webster: "the particular role of an individual species or organism in its community and its environment, including its position in the food cycle and its behavior"). It fails to take account of the fact that, in the words of Jake Patton Beasley in his book

Why We Lose: Why the Black Man/Woman Rest Firmly on the Bottom in America, Africa and Elsewhere, Black people remain at the bottom, oppressed by whites as a class or category. Thus, instead of a change of venue, we may need more a change of niche or a change of genotype to judge us.

Let us explain. Changing venue implies that the new location will be essentially homogeneous in any important respects with the old one (except for the relative paucity of publicity or a priori bias from whatever source that may be pitted against a defendant). The idea of changing venue was made for the agrarian or village society held together by an organic homogeneity, a natural solidarity, where people have essentially the same characteristics. Such a strategy, however, was not designed for the enslaved Blacks. Thus, in the case of the four white police officers who beat Rodney King, changing venue was like jumping out of the skillet into the fire, or out of the chicken coop into the lair of the fox. A change of venue does not help but hurts the hunger for justice, for it glosses over race, class and culture.

With race we confront not only prejudice born of white racism or racial hatred per se, we also run up against new versions of the age-old problem of stereotypes. We are not only despised by the ordinary white individual but misjudged in advance by stereotyped impressions of our life styles and culture. We saw the interplay of stereotype and cultural variations when Mike Tyson's white lawyer attempted to use a Scottsboro Boys defense that purposely painted Tyson in the most animalistic light, causing white male middle-American jurors to doubt his credibility, despite his hard-core background and upbringing, after he said he used a four-letter word to invite Desiree Washington to make love.

When an inner city Black male faces a white middle-class jury, he will have to deal with the well-known fact that most of them will be prejudiced against his very physiognomy. Even white social science literature, said by Black social scientists to

77

be prejudiced against Black people and Black social scientists, stands replete with evidence of the widespread white stereotypes of Blacks. In the course of revealing America's most negative stereotype to be "the Black male criminal," the *Los Angeles Times* (5/31/92) quotes Andrew Hacker, a white professor of political science at Queens College in New York City, as saying "no wonder Black Americans, especially Black men, suffer so much hypertension."

A special *Newsweek* report called "Crime: A Conspiracy of Silence" (5/18/92) stated that "for many Americans, the law-and-order issue is intertwined with unspoken fears about young Black men." They are prone to see even corporate Black men who speak assertively in staff or office deliberations as "hostile" and "threatening." Many whites hesitate to pass a Black male who appears to be low in income walking down the street. White taxicab drivers will pass up a well-dressed Black man, just as policemen will sometimes stop him and search him for no reason at all. A middle-aged Black male psychologist, who has been stopped more than once walking down the street in San Francisco, was apprehended one afternoon by two white policemen. The Black psychologist was dressed in a full dark suit and tie. As he was being searched with his hands up, the police car by chance began to smoke. "Your car is burning," he told the policemen. At that point, one of them walked over to the car and tried to beat out the fire and smoke, while the other continued to frisk the psychotherapist. Suddenly the cop at the car yelled to the other one: "Come over here and help me put out this fire!" "What about him [the suspect]?" the other one said. "He's not the one," the first cop confessed.

A University of Chicago study has reported that 56% of whites believe that Blacks are "prone to violence." Consider the recent newsworthy court case in which Yahweh ben Yahweh, the Black religious leader, was convicted of conspiracy to commit murder. The judge was reported by the *Los Angeles Times* to have instructed the jury of nine whites and three

Blacks: "The majority of the jury is not the same race as the defendant. Please, if you have any biases in that area, rise above them." This is reminiscent of Rodney King's pathetic plea in the middle of the Los Angeles uprising: "Please, can we try to get along? I mean, we're all people here, can we get along?"

Following the announcement of the verdict, the Los Angeles district attorney rushed to retry one of the white officers in the Rodney King beating for the misdemeanor, "excessive force under the cover of authority"—undoubtedly a smokescreen to justify throwing away the key at the four Black males arrested for beating the white truck driver in the heat of the rebellion. Three of the Black men already have been charged with attempted murder. Consider the similarities and differences of the two cases. For example, if the white policemen acted under the cover of authority, the Black defendants were acting under the cover of chaos, under the cover of the moment and the social contagion that gripped those on the scene—even those watching television safely in their homes.

Listen to comments of random participants (as reported in the *Los Angeles Times*):

"Everybody was going in. I just happened to be part of the crowd."

"It was just something everybody was doing."

"I didn't think they'd get me. I was unlucky."

"When they were looting the store, I was just standing there laughing."

The judge handling the retrial of white Officer Powell has rejected the defense attorney's request for change of venue from Los Angeles on the grounds that "potential jurors in this case would have the same state of mind whether they are selected from Los Angeles or another county." While judges are believed to have become more reluctant to grant changes of venue following the Los Angeles uprising, legislators in California and New Jersey, according to the *U.S. News & World Report,* have introduced legislation to ensure that race-related cases "must at least go to sites with similar ethnic populations."

However, it remains apparent that the change of venue, born of the days when there was no television, radio or telephone, is as inadequate as the jury system is obsolete for ensuring a fair and impartial trial for whites, let alone Blacks. All-white juries for Black defendants, or even whites in race-related cases, must be outlawed *because there is no venue in America where a Black man can get a fair and impartial trial from an all-white jury, especially in race-related matters.* When a CNN/*Times* magazine poll asked respondents the question, "What made you angry—the verdict or the violence?" more than twice as many Blacks as whites were angered by the verdict (57 to 21%), while almost three times as many whites were angered more by the violence.

It is the intransigence of white institutional racism, inadequately concealed by the imperatives of an assimilation-crazed era, that generates the despair, resentment and the loss of faith with routine (conventional or institutionalized) means of righting wrongs that historically and repeatedly have exploded in so-called riots. The only difference is that the explosions keep getting bigger and bigger.

NOTES

Our study of so-called race riots began in the early 1960s with the publication of an article in the *Negro History Bulletin* (3/62), "The Day the 'Race Riot' Struck Chicago," which discussed the race riot of 1919 there. Another article appearing in the *Times of London* (7/28/67), "Understanding the Causes of the Black Rebellion," analyzed the summer 1967 Newark and Detroit rebellions. *Fire on Mount Zion* (1990), a book "as told to" us by 94-year-old Mabel B. Little and published by Langston University's M.B. Tolson Collection in collaboration with the Black Think Tank, dealt with the Tulsa riot of 1921. (The Tulsa riot was unique in that white men bombed the Black community—including the majestic Mt. Zion Baptist Church—from small planes.)

We have also been informed by the tools of content analysis acquired in Collective Behavior and Sociology courses (including the Sociology of Jurisprudence) at the University of Chicago, where we first took up the scientific study of race riots. We have employed the following newspapers on a daily basis before, during and since the Los Angeles rebellion: the *Los Angeles Times*, the *New York Times*, the *San Francisco Chronicle* and the *San Francisco Examiner*. Additional accounts and commentaries were examined from the *Norfolk Journal and Guide*, the *Oklahoma Eagle*, the *Sun Reporter*, the *Black Chronicle, Jet, Newsweek, Time* and *U.S. News and World Report*, as well as CNN and the other networks, ABC, NBC, CBS, syndicated and local reports and commentators.

JULIA HARE, ED.D., was named Educator of the Year in Washington, DC by World Book Encyclopedia and the Junior Chamber of Commerce. She has hosted radio programs on KGO, an ABC affiliate in San Francisco, and KSFO, a Golden West Station.

NATHAN HARE, PH.D., coordinated the country's first Black studies program at San Francisco State in 1968. Dr. Hare is the author of *The Black Anglo Saxons* (Third World Press) and co-editor of *Contemporary Black Thought* and *Pan-Africanism*. He is the founding publisher of *The Black Scholar* magazine.

The Hares co-authored: *The Endangered Black Family: Coping with the Unisexualization and Coming Destruction of the Black Race* (1984); *Bringing the Black Boy to Manhood: The Passage* (1985); *Crisis in Black Sexual Politics* (1989); and *Fire on Mount Zion: My Life and History as a Black Woman in America* (1990).

The Symbolism, Logic and Meaning of "Justifiable Homicide" in the 1980s

Frances Cress Welsing

Excerpted from Isis Papers: The Keys to the Colors *(Third World Press), this prophetic essay by Dr. Welsing is included here because of its timeliness, insight and relevance to the Los Angeles rebellion. Ed.*

> Where there is no vision the people will perish.
> —Proverbs 22:1

Black people are afraid, but Black people are going to have to get over their fear. Black people do not know what is happening, but Black people are going to have to learn and understand what is happening. Black people are not thinking, but Black people are going to have to begin thinking. Black people are not being quiet, but Black people are going to have to start getting quiet so they can think. Black people are not analyzing and planning, but Black people are going to have to begin analyzing and planning. Black people do not understand deep self-respect, but Black people are going to have to learn the meaning and practice of deep self-respect. Black people are going to have to stop permitting Black children to play with parenthood. Black people are going to have to stop moaning, rocking, crying, complaining and begging. Black people are going to have to stop thinking that rhyme and rhetoric will solve problems. Black people are going to have to stop finger-popping and singing. Black people are going to have to stop dancing and clowning. Black people are going to have to stop laughing and listening to loud radios. All of these behaviors, and many more, have absolutely nothing to do with addressing the challenges and conditions of the open warfare continuously being waged against the Black collective.

We Black people do not see the war being waged against us because we don't want to and because we are afraid. We are engaging in behavior designed specifically to *block out* any awareness of the war—our true reality. Our behavior thus forces us into the *insanity* of hoping and begging— as opposed to the *sanity* of analysis, specific behavioral pattern design and specific conduct in all areas of people activity: economics, education, entertainment, labor, law, politics, religion, sex and war.

A major strategy in the war against the Black collective is the killing of Black males. Black males are being killed daily, in ever-increasing numbers, across the country. Other non-white males also are being killed in ever-increasing numbers. These Black and other non-white males are being killed by white males in uniforms who have been authorized to carry guns. This particular form of murder and slaughter is called *justifiable homicide.*

Our Black collective today has no greater understanding of this war and the phenomenon of justifiable homicide than it did when Black males were being lynched and castrated daily, 100 years ago in the period of "Reconstruction," or during the reestablishment of white supremacy following the Civil War. Nor does the Black collective have a greater understanding of the current "open hunting season" on Black males than it did two and three decades ago.

The Symbolism, Logic and Meaning of
"Justifiable Homicide" in the 1980s

Because we really do not understand what is going on, in our impotence and ignorance, in our powerlessness and frustration, we start getting mad, fussing, crying, rhyming, begging with picket signs, rioting in misdirection, hooping and hollering, moaning in our churches and preparing again to vote for any white man who smiles at us even though he lies to us. These behaviors are all absolutely useless. Such behaviors are in vain and will take us nowhere. They will all come to naught, and the problem—the war—will simply continue and intensify.

The stage has been reached in our experience of captivity out of Africa wherein we are being challenged to demonstrate a deep self-respect, requiring us to use our whole brain-computers—not just the right side, which permits us to engage in rhetoric, rhythm and rhyme. Now we must begin to exercise and use the left side of our brain-computers, the left cerebral hemisphere, which permits us to analyze critically and decode what is happening daily in front of our eyes and to organize a self- and group-respecting behavioral response to that which the environment is presenting us. We must have a *disciplined* self- and group-respecting response to the specific war being waged against us.

Without critical thinking, however, there is no self-respect. Without self-respect, there is no courage, no self-defense, no justice, no peace and no progress.

In his struggle against white supremacy, the great leader of the Chinese-speaking non-white people, Chairman Mao Tse-Tung, accurately stated as recorded in *The Collective Works of Mao Tse-Tung*, "It is well known that when you do anything, unless you understand its actual circumstances, its nature and its relations to other things, you will not know the laws governing it, or know how to do it, or be able to do it well."

With this in mind, all Black people everywhere must begin to understand the exact and specific nature of the war that is being waged against the Black collective. All Black people must begin to understand in depth *why* we are witnessing Black

85

males being shot dead almost daily by white males in uniforms and why it will soon escalate to more than one per day. Without the specific understanding of why we are seeing this behavior, we are unable to organize behaviors to meet this war strategy effectively.

Furthermore, Black people everywhere must begin to understand why the Black collective, and Black males in particular, have been under intensive attack for the past 2,000 years. Indeed, Jesus was a Black male who was lynched by uniformed white male Roman soldiers 2,000 years ago, a result of the same war that has continued into the present day extension of the same Roman (white) empire.

Whenever there is a sense of increased vulnerability within the local and/or global white collective—as, for example, caused by inflation (currency devaluation), unemployment, loss of a war or counter-struggle by non-white peoples (e.g., Arabs controlling and limiting oil supplies, Iranians taking white hostages, Black guerillas struggling in southern Africa and the loss of the Vietnam War)—there will be an increase of the ever-present "normal" daily slaughter and murder of Black and other non-white males by those both legally and illegally authorized to do so. This murder and slaughter will be *logically* viewed as justified within the specific logic framework of white genetic annihilation.

Within the historic framework of Western civilization and culture (the civilization and culture organized to prevent white genetic annihilation), *all* white people have the spoken or unspoken *mandate* to participate actively in their collective struggle for global white genetic *survival*. This specifically means, of necessity, the murder and slaughter of Black and other non-white males whenever it is felt within the white collective to be necessary and, therefore, justified.

Because Black males, of all non-white males, have the greatest potential to genetically annihilate the white collective, Black males will experience the greatest ferocity of white supremacy's attack through justifiable homicide. Because Black and other non-white males have the potential to produce white genetic annihilation through the use of their genitalia and because genetic annihilation is the most fundamental fear of the global white collective, this collective (consciously or unconsciously) evolved a "counter" *weapon,* or system of weapons, that theoretically could achieve *non-white genetic annihilation.*

The sport of hunting animals (in most instances they have black or dark brown fur) in the white supremacy system/ culture, wherein there is thrill, excitement and pleasure associated with the killing, is the way in which the white collective (most specifically, the white male collective) stays in physical and psychological readiness for killing Black and other non-white males (justifiable homicide), albeit that this obsessive practice may be functioning at unconscious levels of brain-computer activity. Unlike Black and other non-white peoples who killed animals for food and shelter purposes, the white collective engages in this activity as obsessive sport and play. By using the gun (the great equalizer) against helpless animals, they attempt to achieve a sense of manhood and security. A fleeting sense of manhood can be achieved by the white male sports hunter because in killing the large black or brown animal (the symbolic non-white male), there has been a symbolic destruction of the major threat to white genetic survival. Since the achievement, however, is only symbolic, it must be repeated, and so, as soon as the hunting season opens, it is time to hunt again.

In the same period in which there has been an increasing incidence of justifiable homicide, there has also been an increasing enthusiasm for killing helpless animals, making such hunting locations as Potters County, Pennsylvania world famous. White adult males have been taught by their fathers to kill and destroy helpless animals for sport, and in turn, the next generation of white males is taught the means by which to ensure white genetic survival.

Non-white males may say that they also hunt and enjoy hunting, but obviously hunting does not carry the same unconscious meaning for the non-white male as it does for the white male in the context of the global white supremacy. Furthermore, Black males never have gotten a thrill from hunting down white males with dogs and rifles, as has so frequently been practiced by white males against Black males.

It is absolutely critical that all Black people examine and think through the meaning of the following facts: at the very same time Black males are being shot down in the street in ever-increasing numbers, the August 31, 1980 *Washington Post* has reported that Poland, a so-called communist country, already is asking the United States to increase credits for grain purchases from $550 million in the current fiscal year to $670 million in the fiscal year that begins October 1 in order to finance the feed grain it needs to build up meat production. Do "enemies" provide finance for feed grain to build up meat production for one another?

> On August 12, the press reported a West German loan of $672 million designed 'to help bail Poland out of its economic difficulties' (Dusko Doder, the *Washington Post*). On August 22 a consortium led by the Bank of America granted Poland an additional $325 million.
>
> A recent unclassified CIA study reveals that the West has lent Poland a total of $21 billion, the bulk of it in the last five years. The same study reports that the West has lent the Soviet block as a whole an astronomical $78 billion–an amount equal to the total assets of Exxon and General Motors combined. Other experts put the total debt figure well above $100 billion.
>
> Why are we bailing Poland and the Soviet Union out of their economic difficulties, feeding them massive transfusions of hard currency to buy bread for their restive

masses and technology to boost their obsolescent centralized economies? Why are Western banks relieving the USSR of the expensive burden of propping up the Polish economy and regime?

The answer lies in a terse banker's paradox: Make a small loan and you have created a debtor; make a large loan and you have created a partner.

...The $1 billion which Western banks have funneled to Poland during the current crisis is a startling political intervention on behalf of that country's communist regime....

The critical question for Black people is, Who is the real enemy? While massive numbers of Black males are unemployed and increasing numbers are being shot down in the streets in a presumably capitalist country, that same capitalist country is helping white communist countries and their workers return to their jobs and have sufficient meats and other foods on their tables. Basically, the U.S. is supporting the whole white so-called communist block. This does not include the Chinese-speaking non-white peoples.

What is starkly illustrated here is that "capitalism" and "communism" are not two enemies but simply the two extreme ends of the total spectrum of *economic* practices *under* the system of *white supremacy*, wherein the priority is that all whites (males in particular) have jobs whether they are at the right or left *economic* ends of the white supremacy spectrum. The same would be true of the Democratic party/Republican party political spectrum which, in this area of the world, is the total political spectrum of *politics* under white supremacy.

Also, it must be noted that while Black males are being shot down in increasing numbers and experiencing high unemployment, white Cuban communists, in mass numbers, are being admitted to find their places, jobs and housing in this capitalist country and are referred to as "political refugees."

Why L.A. Happened

Black Haitians, however, are not admitted and treated similarly.

In the global white supremacy system, *all* persons classi-
fied as non-white are outside the white power spectrum and are,
in effect, the *real enemy*. Thus, they are manipulated and/or
eliminated at the will of that power system. In the context of
global white supremacy, the only *permanent enemies* are those
persons capable of white genetic annihilation, meaning Blacks
and all other non-white peoples (most specifically males).

In the most narrow perspective, justifiable homicide
refers to the overt shooting murder of a Black male or Black
males by white uniformed male(s). In a broader perspective,
"justifiable homicide" also can refer to the numerous more
subtle tactics of Black male control and destruction. To deny
Black males jobs and genuine upward mobility is to deny them
the functional roles of husband and father. To deny Black
family units functional husbands and fathers on a mass level is
to deny these families stability and to deny male children
models for adult male functioning. Deprivation of male models
for male functioning means permanent Black male social
disfunctioning, affecting all areas of people activity for multiple generations.

The massive increase of Black male bisexuality and
homosexuality to epidemic proportions can be correlated directly to the debased functioning of adult Black males in Black
family units by the racist system. The large number of Black
males engaging in drug use and abuse, including alcohol, also
is tied directly to the severely crippled Black family structure,
brought about through systematically denying Black males
functional roles as husbands and fathers. The massive numbers
of Black males trapped in the juvenile justice system and the
penal system also are related directly to the absence of truly
functional fathers and husbands in the homes from which these
victimized males have come. Current statistics (1980) indicate
that among Blacks, the proportion of one-parent families is a

staggering 49% (1.8 million families). This is 83% higher than a decade ago. Poverty rates among one-parent units are enormously higher than among two-parent units.

The television medium also plays a major role in reinforcing the debasement of the Black male. Bill Cosby is debased by always being depicted conversing at the level of infants. Muhammed Ali is debased by always being shown clowning, chasing roaches and biting into sandwiches instead of watermelons. Sherman Helmsley's character "Mr. Jefferson" in *The Jeffersons* is always clowning, acting like a monkey and climbing over furniture, in spite of supposed superior economic attainment. Mr. Jefferson is contrasted to a more intelligent, manly white male who is married to a Black female (who in real life is married to a white male).

With the massive failure and absence of Black adult male models in family constellations in real life, television provides Black male youths with the white father model of *The White Shadow*, conditioning these children to get used to the absence of Black adult male models and to look up the white adult male as "the man." This theme is advanced further in *Fantasy Island* (starring Herve Vellaichaise) and *Different Strokes* (starring Gary Coleman). Most Black people will look particularly at Gary Coleman and say, "He's a millionaire." However, both Gary Coleman and Herve Vellaichaise are *non-white males* with constitutional and/or genetic deficiencies, causing their physical stature to be abnormally short. Yes, they are indeed excellent actors, but it is their genetic or constitutional abnormality, playing opposite adult white males of normal physical height, that is the core white supremacy presentation in both of these *popular* television series.

The profoundly destructive statement that Black and other non-white males are genetically and constitutionally defective compared to white males is the subtle core message that is being propagated over the airways. This image of non-white male genetic and constitutional abnormality is set forth

Why L.A. Happened

weekly while, as background, newspapers and radios give continuous coverage on the discussion of Nobel Prize winner Dr. William Shockley about the supposed genetic inferiority of Black people and the need for their sterilization. Several years ago, the weekly television presentation and promotion of the Black male as female and transvestite, as portrayed in Flip Wilson's role of "Geraldine," was a similar undermining of the Black male's genetic makeup and masculinity. There was/is no such similar weekly television portrayal of a well-dressed white male as a female and transvestite in the white supremacy system and culture.

Blacks and other non-white people do not perceive these messages because they are blind to the context of the white supremacy power structure that surrounds them. They look at such programs and are pleased; they smile and laugh. Nonetheless, this continued presentation of Black genetic inferiority makes the final destruction of Blacks appear to Blacks themselves as a relief from the burden of their own genetic inadequacy. One can be assured that there will *never* be a weekly television presentation of a constitutionally and genetically deformed blue-eyed, blond *white male* playing opposite an intelligently behaving Black male of normal stature, as long as the white supremacy system remains intact.

These more subtle means of achieving justifiable homicide all serve to advance the ultimate goal of white genetic survival. For, with Black adult males unable to function as men (on drugs, in prison, as clowns and buffoons, as infants and perceived as genetic defectives, transvestites and homosexuals), there will not be a major threat of white genetic annihilation, and white genetic survival is assured. The white collective cannot be asked to cease their drive for justifiable homicide in its gross and subtle forms. To do so would mean white suicide.

It is, therefore, the self-respecting task of Blacks and all other non-whites to understand the war and the behavioral dynamic of white supremacy in which they are presently trapped. Through this understanding, we must evolve our own behavior (in all areas of people activity) that will eventually checkmate this global white necessity and injustice.

Black people may begin by educating all Black male children to understand white supremacy and by putting increased pressure on Black males to recognize their role as husbands and fathers. This understanding means that Black men must work and provide support for their families, which the white collective attempts to prevent them from doing. Males who do not demand and fight, if necessary, to have jobs cannot become husbands or fathers. Most certainly, teenage male children cannot become parents, which means that Black females will have to learn when and under what circumstances they should relate to Black males in the act of sexual intercourse and self-reproduction.

This internal pressure to preserve the role of Black manhood becomes a means by which the concept of Black manhood is developed and preserved by Black peoples themselves. This activity will counter the thrust of the Black male as female, clown, infant, buffoon, transvestite, homosexual. Black males who are unwilling to fight for their manhood are thereby indicating that they debase Black manhood and will not be able to teach it to the next generation. These males do not deserve the privilege of procreating themselves, and this should be enforced by all Black females who are self-respecting.

White supremacy is war against Black people in general and against Black males in particular, as embodied in such tactics and strategies as justifiable homicide. It will require a total commitment and counter-war effort on the part of all Black peoples to neutralize, by every means at their disposal, this war of racist injustice.

As Black people, we also can adopt the definition that under the conditions of white supremacy, Black manhood does not mean macho or money, but instead it means *warrior* or *soldier* against white supremacy, embracing everything that the words warrior or soldier imply. Those who do not wish to be warriors or soldiers should not procreate themselves, as their offspring can be expected to be destroyed by white supremacy anyway. This is by no means a definitive statement on Black response to justifiable homicide, but it is an attempt to elevate the discussion on this specific white supremacy war strategy. Further discussion among Black people will help to define all necessary Black behavioral responses.

DR. FRANCES CRESS WELSING is formerly an Assistant Professor of Pediatrics and Adjunct Professor of Social Work at Howard University. She is currently a medical officer at the Department of Human Resources, Mental Health Administration, and Clinical Director for the Paul Robeson School for Growth and Development, Washington, DC. Her definitive work, *The Isis Papers: The Keys to the Colors*, was published by Third World Press.

Missing Movement, Missing Fathers:
The Culture of Short Lives and
Low Expectations
Haki R. Madhubuti

I entered adulthood in the '60s right out of the U.S. army into the streets of Chicago to be absorbed by the Black Arts/Civil Rights/Black Power movements. Those movements saved my life and gave greater meaning and cultural* purpose to me, a young Black man fresh out of the military. Most of my life I had been subtly taught to hate myself and my people, and for the three years of military service, I had also been taught to kill people who looked like me.

---

*I am using *culture* to denote a working system of values, attitudes and institutions (family to U.S. government) that influences individual and group behavior in all areas of human activity: law, education, arts, politics, agriculture, language, military, sports, entertainment, health, economics and social development.

Why L.A. Happened

This movement, which encompassed all of the '60s and part of the '70s, cannot be dismissed by draft-dodging vice presidents and self-righteous politicians born with privilege in their oatmeal. Tons of revisionist historians and political scientists are now trying to paint the movements of the '60s as destructive forces in American life. This may indeed be a serious consideration from their point of view. However, most participants felt that the struggle to share local, state and federal power; the opening up of public facilities to all on an equal basis; the empowering of the disenfranchised with the vote; the recapturing and redefining of the Black/African image in the American/world mind; the equal participation in the educational process by the underserved; the enlargement of living and work space for people of color; the redefinition of what it means to be a woman in a male dominant society; and the open and raw disclosures of the worldwide destructive powers of racism (white world supremacy) in maintaining a nazi-like world from South Africa to South Carolina is what the Black movement of the '60s and early '70s was about.

The Rodney King incident pre- and post-beating verdict only helps to sharpen our focus on the political reality of young Black men in today's America. Obviously, one's perspective is always open to question. The difference between knowing and not knowing in a cultural/political context in the United States is a larger question than just the quality of one's formal education. This is why the Black movement was so important and instrumental in the political/cultural development of millions of people; it gave us a context to find and investigate content. If nothing else, we learned the right questions to ask. The battle lines were not always clear, it was not always white vs. Black, white Christians vs. Black Christians vs. Black Muslims vs. Jews, Black politicians vs. Black activists, negro vs. Black vs. African, capitalists vs. socialists vs. communists —and we can go on and on. The complexity of Black struggle has always been at the heart of our reactions. W.E.B. Du Bois in his groundbreaking *The Souls of Black Folk* to Harold Cruse's *The Crisis of the Negro Intellectual* to Frances Welsing's *Isis Papers* all delineate the difficulty in deciding "a way" to move a people from "enslavement" to liberation.

However, the major point is that the Black movement provided young African Americans of that period a context for discovering identity and purpose, and it also provided serious proposals for the future. The movement prevented many young women and men from being swallowed by the ever-present lowest common denominator: street culture. This movement existed as extended family, developing a culture that was productive and caring. It provided young people with something to care about that was not insulting to their own personhood. It defined relationships and challenged us to defend our own limited resources. But one of the major contributions was in the arena of *ideas*.

For the first time in the lives of many of us, we were comforted with ethical, moral, spiritual, political, historical and economic questions and dilemmas. We, through our day-to-day activities, were forced to think at another level about the United States and the world. Often our lives depended upon the quality of our thinking and decisions. This *critical* thinking at such a young age matured many of us, and we began to see our struggle as one deeply attached to international realities and liberation struggles in other parts of the world. We were reading, on our own, the works of Carter G. Woodson, Frantz Fanon, Amical Cabral, E. Franklin Frazier, Gwendolyn Brooks, Margaret Walker, Richard Wright, John O. Killens, Kwame Nkrumah, Julius Nyerere, Marcus Garvey and others.

The Black movement doesn't exist today as it did in the '60s. This is not to suggest that there are no movements. The profound difference between the '60s and today is that no national Black political movement exists of any consequence. Even then there were many streams, but there was only one river. There existed a national consensus on broadly defined goals and objectives. Whether one worked in the NAACP, CORE, SNCC, SCLC, the Urban League, NOI, Black Panther Party, US Organization, CAP or the Black Arts and Southern Student Movements,* one had a connection, a force, a greater purpose than one's personal geography, which often defined us.

The political and cultural realities of today are just as oppressive as the past, but the vehicle to combat them does not exist at a national level. We are fighting the same battles, but our movement has been torn asunder, and most of the young are not being nurtured into struggle at a responsible level. Many young people who are industrious do find local organizations, and there still are socially committed churches in which to work. However, the great majority of youth find themselves seeking answers in the streets.

During the '60s, whether our national spokesperson was Martin Luther King, Malcolm X, Stokley Carmichael (now Kwame Toure) or Angela Davis, there was a feeling of "going together" and of watching each others' backs. It didn't matter too much if one wore African-centered dress, a suit, a suit and bow tie or overalls, the movement kept many of us busy and working for a higher goal. This movement minimized gang, drug and criminal activity in our communities. That such a movement doesn't exist today speaks loudly to *our* failure as a people to develop a *leadership* who understands the force and power of national organizations that function around the power of ideas rather than egos. This leadership has not developed replacements that it can support and guide. This short-sighted-

---

*National Association for the Advancement of Colored People, Congress on Racial Equality, Student Nonviolent Coordinating Committee, Southern Christian Leadership Conference, Nation of Islam, Congress of African People.

ness has left most young men and women with no alternative for survival than going to the streets.

Street culture is a culture of containment, and most young people do not realize that it is too often a dead end. *Street culture*, as I am using the term, is a counter-force to *movement culture*. Street culture in today's urban reality denotes survival at all cost. This is mostly negative because it demands constant adjusting to circumstances that are often beyond young people's control or understanding: economics, education, housing, jobs, food, law, etc. In urban America, traveling to and from school, church, work, welfare offices or recreation can be and often are life and death choices for young people, mainly young males. There is no national or local political/cultural-Black/Latino movement to direct or protect our youth today.

FATHERS AND FAMILY

I believe and maintain that if culturally focused/politically clear and responsible Black fathers were a majority in the African-American family and community, there would not be a gang, drug or crime problem at the level that exists today. This is not to suggest that gangs, drugs or crime would not exist in our communities, but it is to state that gangs, drugs and crime would not rule or run our communities as they now do in too many instances. Fathers in working families *do* make a difference; Black women against great odds are fighting a losing battle, and responsible and dependable fathers, grandfathers, uncles and men of our extended family are critically needed.

One need not go back over the statistics detailing the decline of Black children born into two-parent households. The figures do not speak well of the Black community. Marriage, whether "legal" (sanctioned by the courts), or common law (people deciding to live together without legal documents), is on the decline. However, the babies do not stop coming, and the *music* and *love* so badly needed in the rearing of children are disappearing quickly in the African-American community.

Stable families and communities are absolutely necessary if we are to have productive and loving individuals. Marriage represents the foundation of family. Without marriage (that is, some bonding tradition that sanctions and forces "partners" into commitments beyond the bedroom), families would soon die; or other types of families would form. Families are the foundation for community. Like a family, a functional community provides security, caring, wealth, resources, cultural institutions, education, employment, a spiritual force, shelter and a challenging atmosphere. Families and community shape the individual into a productive or non-productive person. Without family, without community, individuals are left to "everything is everything," and if "everything is everything," "nothing is nothing."

Fathers are the missing links in the lives of many young African Americans. In an increasingly dangerous and unpredictable world, absent fathers add tremendously to the insecurity of children. It is common knowledge that children function best in an atmosphere where both parents combine and compliment their energies and talents in the rearing of children. Even if pregnancy is an accident, it is clear that once a decision is made to bring a child to term, the rearing of that child cannot be accidental. Most children are born at the top of their game, *genius level*. It is the socialization process that turns most creative, talented and normal children into dependent and helpless adults.

In a patriarchal society, Black men must be able to offer their families a measurement of protection and, at a minimum, basic life-giving needs, such as clothing, shelter, food, education and security. The West and most of the world define manhood as the ability to protect and provide for one's family. If a man doesn't do that, according to most cultures, he is incomplete (i.e., not a man). A good many Black men are not able to deliver in these two areas. Here are some of the reasons:

1. White world supremacy (racism)—Black men are the major threat to white male rule.
2. Failure of integration—Many Black men believe(d) America's big lie of the melting pot theory.
3. Failure of national and local welfare system—the development of a beggar's mentality among many Black people.
4. Failure of public education.
5. Changing economic system—increased dependency on the state.
6. Our replacement in the market place by white women and teenagers.
7. Loss of self-respect, self-esteem and self-love.
8. Ignorance of one's own history and accomplishments.
9. Unawareness of changing world realities.
10. Lack of skills—especially business skills.
11. Fear.

For conscious men, none of this should be new. However, in this *war* situation that we live in, the circumstances demand that Black men rise to the *challenge*. And a great part of that challenge is to be responsible husbands and fathers. Without both, a bright future is doubtful. Being a good and fruitful husband and father may be the most *difficult task facing African American men*.

We now live in a time, a first in our history, when there are millions of African-American children with absent fathers. Other than the period of chattel slavery, there has never been a time when the absence of Black fathers has been so grim. This tide of absent, unavailable, nonfunctioning fathers must be reversed. There are *no easy solutions*.

Fathering for most Black men is learned on the job. Generally, by that time, for many fathers it is too late. There are few classes in fathering. However, fathering *is* taught; it's a learned process. Most Black men give very little thought to the

101

Why L.A. Happened

lifelong commitment that fathers *must* make to their children.

Children learn to do most things by watching and imitating their parents or care-givers. Formal education starts generally at the age of five for most children and at two and a half for the blessed few who are able to benefit from Headstart or private schools. Children learn to be mothers or fathers by observing and studying their mothers, fathers, grandparents, aunts, uncles and television.

These days most Black boys learn to be fathers by watching the wind (i.e., spaces reserved for missing fathers). Many of them also receive instruction in fathering from their mothers' discussions about absent "dads" or whatever names these men are given. If there is anything clear about the African-American community, it is that women are having serious difficulty teaching Black boys to be men and, by extension, to be fathers.

However, this is not a condemnation of Black women who are trying, against great odds, to raise their sons into responsible and recognizable Black men. The facts suggest that many of them are not succeeding, and the facts also suggest that it is *ignorant, stupid* and *insensitive* to blame Black women for not *raising strong Black men*. The music in these women's lives is little, and to be left alone to raise the children may be an impossible task for many of them. However, we do know that millions of African-American women do rise to the challenge and are responsible for millions of Black men who have made "successful" transitions from boyhood to manhood.

Again, it is not easy. There is a difference between raising children and rearing them. Mari Evans, in a very important paper, "The Relationship of Child-Rearing Practices to Chaos and Change in the African American Family," states:

> ...raising [children] is "providing for," while rearing is "responding to." Raising can be satisfied by providing the essentials: food, shelter, clothing and reasonable care. "Rearing" is a carefully thought out process.

Missing Movement, Missing Fathers:
The Culture of Short Lives and Low Expectations

Rearing begins with a goal and is supported by a clear view of what are facts and what is truth (and the two are not necessarily synonymous). Rearing is complex and requires sacrifice and dedication. It is an ongoing process of "preparation." Joe Kennedy reared presidents; the British royal family rears heirs to the English throne; and when a young African doctor, born in the continent and presently in self-exile in a neighboring country because of her ANC (African National Congress) commitment was interviewed on the news recently and was asked if she was not afraid for her four-year-old son, given her political activism, said, "He has a duty to lay down his life for his people," she announced the rearing of a "race man."...Obviously something different, some carefully thought out process, some long-range political view is present when one has a clear sense of one's own reality and therefore intends to rear presidents, rulers, or free men and women.

I think that Mari Evans, in her own unique and poetic manner, has set forth the challenge for African-American people, the rearing of "race men and women."

If fathers give some thought to this, it should become clear that fathering (i.e., parenting) is also a political act. As a colonized people fighting for survival and development, African Americans must see our children as future "warriors" in this struggle for liberation. Mari Evans defined colonization as "suppression and exploitation designed to keep a people powerless, dependent, subordinate, and mystified." Again, we are at war for the minds, bodies, souls, spirits and futures of our children. Ms. Evans states it this way: "Child-rearing should be the primary concern of an oppressed people, and although the rearing of race men and women is obviously a stressful, complex and tedious process, it should be entered into at birth."

I want to make it clear that we Black men cannot depend on others to do our job. Fathering must be as important to us as love-making (sex). It is easy to make babies but difficult to rear them. In my book, *Black Men: Obsolete, Single, Danger-*

Why L.A. Happened

ous? The Afrikan American Family in Transition, I write about this subject in greater detail.

The rebellions in L.A. and other cities in the country were not aberrations but unsophisticated and uncoordinated reactions to injustice and political/economic frustrations. Street culture took over and guided much of the response to the Simi Valley decision. When a community doesn't have culturally conscious and committed institutions—family, church, political and economic—in a time of stress, crisis or calm, it is left to its own survival instincts. In this case, the streets won, we lost, confusing our expectations and shortening many of our lives.

HAKI R. MADHUBUTI is Publisher/Editor of Third World Press. He is a professor of English and Director of the Gwendolyn Brooks Center for Black Literature and Creative Writing at Chicago State University. In 1991, he was awarded an American Book Award and was named author of the year by the Illinois Council of Teachers of English. His book, *Black Men: Obsolete, Single, Dangerous? The Afrikan American Family in Transition*, remains one of the top 10 best sellers among Black writers in the country. Primarily a poet, he is completing a book length autobiographical poem and a follow-up book to *Black Men—Claiming Earth*—to be published in 1993.

Violence, Doublespeak and the American Ruling Elite

Bakari Kitwana

> What counts today, the question which is looming on the horizon, is the need for a redistribution of wealth. Humanity must reply to this question or be shaken to pieces.
> —Frantz Fanon, *The Wretched of the Earth*

> The whole structure of America must be changed. We are engaged in a class struggle...We are dealing with the gulf between the have and the have-nots.
> —Martin Luther King, *Where Do We Go From Here*

Many Americans were shocked by the rebellion that erupted in Los Angeles, and in other cities throughout the country on a smaller scale, when the four white police officers who violently beat Rodney King during an arrest for a traffic violation were acquitted on all charges of excessive force. The American economic elite has done much in the way of disseminating misinformation to maintain middle-class and poor contentment.[1] Yet, the continuing obsession of this white ruling elite to dominate wealth, property, power and resources necessitates the heightening of repression: in this case, the public display of judicial injustice.

Why L.A. Happened

All Americans were forced to confront the reality that African Americans do not obtain justice under the law. Despite the immediate contradiction this poses to the American ideal of "liberty and justice for all," the elite hoped, by the use of the usual doublespeak and propaganda—in conjunction with the firmly entrenched Americanization process—that people would merely express disappointment and ignore the far-reaching ramifications of this verdict. However, at this juncture, business as usual and contentment were not the outcome, and for those who have paid close attention to the economic elite's historical development, their tremendous growth in wealth over the past decade and the continuing conditions that produced the uprising, such rebellions are inevitable. In fact, as the economic elite continues its unending quest to accumulate capital and, in turn, heighten the repression, we should look for, at minimum, additional spontaneous rebellions. The rebellions may appear isolated and will be described as such by the elite and their institutions, but all explosions will seek to address a larger problem.

The Federal Reserve, in conjunction with the Internal Revenue Service, recently completed a report which indicated that "by 1989, the top 1 percent (834,000 households with about $5.7 trillion net worth) was worth more than the bottom 90 percent of Americans (94 million households with about $4.8 trillion in net worth)."[2] This economic elite "accounted for 37 percent of private net worth in 1989 up from 31 percent in 1983."[3] What is even more striking is the fact that the increase of the top 0.5% "people with wealth in the tens and hundreds of million dollars"[4]) of this 1% was even more dramatic, suggesting the elite is becoming more and more concentrated.

The increases in wealth, in part, were influenced by increases in income. According to the Congressional Budget Office, this 1% economic elite had the greatest gains in family income (70%) during the late 1970s and the 1980s.[5] If income gains had been equally distributed throughout all class levels, only 7% of the increase would have gone to the economic elite.[6] These income gains were also affected by enormous income tax rate cuts that emerged during the Reagan years, where the top rate went from 70 to 28%. (Today the top rate is 31%.) Thus, the elite paid, on average, only 27% of their income to the Internal Revenue Service; in 1977 they paid 36%.[7] Income alone does not account for the disparity between rich and poor. Additionally, the inherited wealth of the top 1% also increased between 1979 and 1988 from 67.5 to 73.1%.[8]

All of these studies complement this year's Economic Report of the President which agrees that the elite enjoyed greater gains in the past decade and that poverty increased from 1979 to 1989.[9] The conditions for the poor look more and more bleak as current reports from the Center for Budget and Policy Priorities (which reported that "between 1977 and 1988, the average after-tax income of the top fifth of the population rose by 34 percent, while the bottom fifth's current share fell 10 percent"[10]), the Children's Defense Fund as well as the U.S. Census Bureau[11] all highlight the disparity between America's super-rich and the majority poor.

The existence of a white economic elite class in America has been adequately discussed and documented.[12] However, these recent reports suggest that this disparity is becoming even greater as the rich become a smaller, more concentrated elite class and the poor account for an overwhelming majority. These numbers and percentages speak volumes about the state of affairs for the American poor, with a large segment of the African-American community falling into this class. For an individual living alone, the poverty rate in 1990 was $6,652, "$10,419 for a family of three and 13,359 for a family of four."[13] As an indication of how the poor are forced to live, keep in mind that annual income for a minimum wage full-time job is under $9,000 (gross). Given that 70% of this is spent on shelter (according to the Children's Defense Fund[14]), imagine surviving on this income or less! In fact, when the extremely low threshold for the poverty level is examined in a realistic context, many of those considered lower-middle class face dire conditions, and those in the middle- and upper-middle classes know they are one paycheck away from the underclass. In short, the studies highlight the need to explore alternative economic systems for human development and ownership of resources to resolve the problems of extreme poverty, homelessness, unemployment, inadequate health care, ineffective education, etc., faced by the majority.

The continuing existence of an economic elite class in America which profits from the majority poor underclass mocks the American ideals of equality, people's freedom and democracy. Add America's ongoing racial conflict to the equation and the dynamics intensify. White supremacy is encouraged among whites, while Black acceptance of inhumane treatment is nurtured via American institutions.[15] Many whites have come to believe that the violation of Black life is acceptable because of the myths of white superiority and Black inferiority endorsed by societal institutions. According to Dr. Frances Cress Welsing, Black life is violated in hopes of making white life (by contrast) appear more valuable. This is carried out "in all areas of human activity (economics, education, entertainment, labor, law, politics, religion, sex and war)."[16] The highly frequent occurrence and acceptance of this practice establishes it as "the norm." Given these realities, the Simi Valley verdict was nurtured by the society, and the ruling elite hoped that Black acceptance of "the normal" would again dictate Black acceptance of the verdict.

The Rodney King incident is not a rarity. White police beatings of Black citizens occur regularly and have initiated many of America's major race riots. The number of Blacks and

Hispanics killed by the police and National Guard has been continuously downplayed, but as early as May 1, 1992, at least 10 people had been killed by "law enforcers."[17] Further, a significant percentage of those killed during the rebellion were shot in the head, which would require a certain level of marksmanship not typical of an amateur. After the rebellion, Stacy Koon (one of the tried officers) stated, "you have to be able to rationalize the violence you use...you dehumanize the suspect." The language reveals much about the American perception of Black people. To him, just as Blacks are perceived in general in the white supremacist framework, Rodney King is subhuman and as such can be beaten mercilessly.

The white ruling elite, whose interests are most effectively achieved through the economic system that reinforces the existing institutionalized sexism, classism and racism, exert exordinant influence over American institutions. Their values and ideas are infused in institutions that represent and sustain American culture and are important tools used to maintain their power.[18] Thus, the power elite's ideals of Blacks and the valuelessness of Black life are part of the culture. The police are only one vehicle (and an important one) by which this idea is brought into existence and maintained. The police's use of violence becomes not only justifiable but acceptable and not to be questioned—even when people observe the injustice with their own eyes.

Recognizing these realities of race and class and how they affect the quality of Black life in America, George Jackson precisely described the average person who is counted among the bottom 90% of America's households. His analysis gets to the core of the life reality for the poor underclass.

> The slave...Born to a premature death, a menial, subsistence-wage worker, odd-job man, the cleaner, the caught, the man under hatches, without bail—that's me, the

colonial victim. Anyone who can pass the civil service examination today can kill me tomorrow. Anyone who passed the civil service examination yesterday can kill me today with complete immunity.[19]

How does American society begin to effectively deal with this reality? Because the accumulation of wealth is their priority, the elite fail to approach the problems of the poor with effective solutions. Statements made by members of the ruling elite following the uprising suggest this conflict of interest and indicate that they would like to get on with business as usual. President George Bush stated in his address on May 1, 1992 following the uprising that "violence will end, justice will prevail." This statement ignores the violence used by the state and the denial of justice to the poor—both to maintain the elite class and their privilege. Likewise, an "anonymous" senior Republican strategist encouraged Bush not to publicly get involved in discussions of racial injustice or the underclass. "They are not our issues,"[20] he said. Republican presidential candidate Patrick Buchanan on Jesse Jackson's CNN program, *Both Sides* (5/2/92), argued that the rioters must be "prosecuted to the full extent of the law," making no comment on the issue of poverty and the imbalance of wealth. He even went as far as to describe Los Angeles as one of the richest cities in the country to disprove the argument that poverty was a reason for the rebellion. Yet, in March, unemployment in California (which, according to the UCLA Business Forecasting Project, has steadily increased since 1989, as personal income has declined) was well above the 7.3% national rate at 8.5%.[21] Further, California lost approximately 330,000 jobs both in 1990 and 1991,[22] respectively; and job availability continues to decline, as various industries are depressed while others forecast difficulty.

Additionally, comments from petty bougouisie conservatives who perceive the ruling elite's interest as their own were hoped to confuse the poor and add credibility to the state's response. Former L.A. police chief Darryl Gates' remarks to members of the National Guard on a *60 Minutes* broadcast (5/5/92)—"we thank you for your help in putting those SOB's in jail where they belong"—demonstrate that he does not identify with the source of the people's rage and fails to view the rebellion in its political context. Likewise, Walter Williams (who is Black), perhaps motivated by his confusion that he too can share the elite's status, said, "the rioting and looting in Los Angeles should have been met with strict shoot-to-kill orders."[23]

Clearly, more effective alternatives must be explored. Presently, the state's method of maintaining disparities between rich and poor, as well as between Black and white, has been violence. Despite the state's denouncement of violence in the aftermath of the Simi Valley verdict, the primary means of maintaining this "law and order" is violence, brute force, in the tradition of Rodney King. Yet, it is not necessary for the beatings to occur daily (although they do), just that people know that they can and will happen, and the police involved will commit such crimes "with complete immunity."

The police are the first line of defense between the elite and the poor; their role, as perceived by the distinctive groups, is not identical. For the elite, the police protect property, their investments, and exist primarily to remind the "slaves" of their powerlessness, to remind the slaves (those in the 90 percentile) that any attempt to resist their station by any means other than "law and order," despite its ineffectiveness, will be met with violence. The Black poor recognize this, and to them, the police as an instituition represent repression and violence unbound, as they parade throughout the inner city (occupied territory). Frantz Fanon described this juxtaposition this way:

> It is obvious that the agents of government speak the
> language of pure force. The intermediary does not

111

lighten the oppression, nor seek to hide the domination; he shows them up and puts them into practice with the clear conscience of the upholder of the peace; yet he is the bringer of violence into the home and mind of the native. [24]

However, "violence," H. Rapp Brown stated, "is as American as apple pie." The presence of the national guard, army and police in Los Angeles, in addition to the United States' military instigation and involvement internationally, is indicative of that. Likewise, Black-white interaction historically has been marked by white-on-Black violence.[25] The number of "law enforcers" dispatched to end the rebellion was at least an absurd 26,450 (8000 Los Angeles city police, 8000 Los Angeles County sheriff's police, 750 additional highway patrol officers,[26] 4000 National Guard, 1200 federal law officers and 4500 Army and Marine soldiers).[27]

White-on-Black violence as a form of repression does not begin or end with enforcement agencies (whether it manifests in unjust imprisonment, police brutality or political assassination)[28] but occurs psychologically on many other levels. From preschool through graduate study, the American educational experience is marked by violence. The ongoing terroristic immersion of African Americans into European culture is an extremely violent encounter that affects all areas of Black life.[29] This seasoning/whitening process becomes even more dramatic in the face of heightening Black consciousness: the violent process of miseducation intensifies for Black youth, many of whom are immersed in hip hop culture and listen daily to Boogie Down Productions ("the barbarian teaches us to hate our roots. Despise our culture, look for culture in another man's existence. Resistance. Resist this master plan, to turn the Black man into a statistic."[30]), Ice Cube ("Do I have to sell me a whole lot of crack, for decent shelter and clothes on my back? Or should I just wait for help from Bush or Jesse Jackson and

Operation Push?"[31]) and others declaring on another level "stop the violence." Also, with the continuing pressure to incorporate Black studies into the curriculum, particularly in urban settings where Black student populations are the overwhelming majority, the defense of white studies as universal[32] and the antagonism toward the search for higher political consciousness through education must be confronted.

Similarly, the display of violence in movies and news broadcasts desensitizes many and de-emphasizes the extent that violence maintains the status quo, as the state's violence is characterized as "law and order" and "protecting democracy," while "violence" and "terrorism" are the words used to describe activity that rebels against the existing social order; and the victims are depicted as the unruly criminal element in need of rehabilitation via imprisonment.

This relationship of violence, classism and racism produces unjust living conditions for the majority poor. The frustration, powerlessness and hopelessness that the people face intensify under recessionary trends that force the poor into survival beyond already below subsistence conditions. The Labor Department estimated that at least 2.2 million payroll jobs have been lost since June 1990.[33] Nationally, among others, the following companies contributed to this workers nightmare: General Motors (laid off 70,000+), IBM (20,000+), Pan Am (10,000+) and Midway Airlines (4500+). Unlike past recessions, the service industry cannot serve as a buffer for these cutbacks. (Between August 1990 and Feburary 1991, approximately 208,000 jobs were lost in the service industry.[34]) These extensive cutbacks immediately affect workers in the 90 percentile.

As the conditions worsen, people must explore alternative means of day-to-day survival. Often this means turning to an underground economy.[35] The response from the state is the further heightening of repression: the institutionalization of additional practices that violate the human rights of the poor and "middle class," beyond already institutionalized methodologies of miseducation, ineffective political processes, judicial injustice, etc.

The reversal of Affirmative Action policies, the dedication of federal and state governments to building bigger and more prisons to "hold" the poor underclass, as well as the considerable cutbacks in welfare assistance are all examples of what the future holds. Similarly, the federal and state collaboration on "weed and seed" programs for sweeping low-income housing projects—where residents and their guests are illegally searched and harassed[36]—and the FBI's instigation of conflict between rival gangs (in the tradition of COINTELPRO), in addition to further policing the displaced underclass (explored through such methods as the city of Chicago's tentative non-loitering ordinance) insist that repression is here.

Yet the heightening of repression raises consciousness.

The poor recognize their powerlessness and seek redress first against each other.[37] However, when the repression is undeniable, unbearable and demands confrontation, political consciousness is raised and violence is revisited upon those who exploit the people in daily interaction—the police as well as other ethnic groups that set up stores in the Black community, some of whom treat Blacks unfairly and in a despicable fashion. Very eloquent and profound man-on-the-street interviews broadcasted on CNN, *60 Minutes* and *Nightline* during and after the rebellion, as well as the rarely publicized attacks on police and activity directed toward specific ethnic groups, are indicative of the growing consciousness. George Jackson best articulated this moment of truth in his searing account describing the need for people's war, a violent overthrow of a government that does not function in the majority's best interest:

> I've lived with repression all my life, a repression so
> formidable that any movement on my part can only bring
> relief, the respite of a small victory or the release of
> death.[38]

L.A. happened because people cannot live incomplete
lives while observing daily (most often via the media) those
who control much of the country's wealth and resources and
who therefore have the influence needed to enhance the lives of
the poor but do very little in fear of losing privileges. The
disparity between bantustans in South Africa and white communities surrounding Johannesburg is no more than that between Beverly Hills and South Central Los Angeles. While
America parades internationally as the keeper of the peace and
leader of the "free" world, the psychological effects on America's
poor are overwhelmingly destructive. Continued maintenance
of these conditions with no redress is ultimately debilitating.
The economic and political elite habitually fail to institute
effective policies to meet the needs of the poor. The elite will
do whatever is necessary to avoid the question of wealth
redistribution to accomodate the rest of the country. The
important thing is to maintain the privileges. The poor, who
know powerlessness, homelessness, unemployment, etc., do
not even approach the proverbial "American Dream," particularly the Black poor, who know that white racism ignores class
status. As the repression continues, the middle class and poor
will feel more and more like outcasts, particularly as the rich are
prospering. Now is the time when the people should demand
a redistribution of wealth. Yet the rich get richer as the poor
suffer under recessionary trends, and no "leader" seriously
challenges this.

What are the people to do? Carry out their frustration
instantaneously? Yes! But, when do African Americans move
beyond the riot phase (a phase we have lingered in far too long)?

115

Why L.A. Happened

What will it take for the American poor to challenge the ruling elite's government and backward *isms* at a more sophisticated level? What will it take for African Americans to begin to counter the terrorism being inflicted daily? When will we begin to look at the Palestinian-Israeli conflict as a varied display of the dynamics of racism, sexism and classism that we confront? The Palestinians who resist are not "terrrorists." They are people who recognize a ruling class' imposition of inhumane and unequal treatment despite United Nations approval. What will it take for African Americans to arrive at this level? Beyond intellectual resistance, although it is necessary, beyond institution building, although it is necessary, beyond ressurecting cultural values and deprograming the imposed miseducation, beyond all this to the unavoidable and necessary confrontation with the source of the real problem at the "real" level!

At times like these, the ruling elite's private ownership of wealth must be challenged as never before. The challenge must move beyond rhetoric and slogans to the language of communication most familiar to the power elite: just as violence maintains the imbalanced distribution of wealth, violence is needed to institute change. After decades of persistent agitation against repression, it is evident that economic change for the masses will come no other way. The attempt by some politicians to revamp health care policies to benefit all of America's people is a step in the right direction. The movement toward multiculturalism so that particular ethnic groups are brought in contact with the best that their people have produced as part of their educational experience is also helpful. However, the elite stand strongly opposed to both of these agendas. From their perspective, it is politically incorrect for all people, despite income level, to have access to even basic medical assistance that would tremendously enhance their lives and for people of color to access their own culture. With their historically unswerving stance in maintaining their position in America, it is not likely that America's elite will establish a just and equal society.

America's greatest problem is not high unemployment, poverty or homelessness, although seriously focusing in on these issues will direct us toward the solutions. The real problem is white economic elite rule—as well as its violence and doublespeak—that must be disrupted to begin to approach the difficulties faced by those in the 90 percentile, particularly the ever-increasing underclass. People can reflect on the rebellion as a starting point in history to move toward a more fair and just society, socially and economically, or we can be lulled to sleep by the elite's rhetoric and wane back into contentment. But certainly, until this elite is confronted, violence, doublespeak and repression will continue, and police beatings and judicial injustice will persist as solutions are explored within a framework constructed and maintained by the perpetrators of the problems.

NOTES

1.   Noam Chomsky, *Neccesary Illusions: Thought Control in Democratic Societies* (South End Press, 1989).

2.   Sylvia Nasar, *New York Times*, "Fed Report Gives New Data on Gains By Richest in 80's" (April 21, 1992) p. 1.

3.   *Ibid.*

4.   Gene Koretz, *Business Week*, "Would the Economy Gain From Spreading Inherited Wealth?" (May 18, 1992) p. 22.

5.   Sylvia Nasar, *New York Times*, "Who Paid the Most Taxes in the 80's? The Superrich" (May 31, 1992) p. 4.

6.   Sylvia Nasar, *New York Times*, "However You Slice the Data The Richest Did Get Richer" (May 11, 1992) C2.

7.   Sylvia Nasar, *New York Times*, "Who Paid the Most Taxes in the 80's? The Superrich" (May 31, 1992) p. 4.

8.   Holly Sklar, *Z Magazine*, "Washington, DC Divide and Conquer" (March 1992) p. 13.

9.   Sylvia Nasar, *New York Times*, "However You Slice The

Data the Richest Did get Richer" (May 11, 1992) p. C2.

10. Holly Sklar, *Z Magazine*, "Washington DC, Divide and Conquer" (March 1992) p. 14-15.

11. *Ibid.*

12. Noam Chomsky, *The Culture of Terrorism* (South End Press, 1988) and Sidney Willhelm, *Who Needs the Negro?* (Third World Press, 1993).

13. Holly Sklar, *Z Magazine*, "Washington DC, Divide and Conquer" (March 1992) p. 14.

14. *Ibid.*

15. Haki Madhubuti, *Black Men: Obsolete; Single, Dangerous?* (Third World Press, 1990) and Frances Cress Welsing, *The Isis Papers: The Keys to the Colors* (Third World Press, 1991).

16. Frances Cress Welsing, *The Isis Papers*, p. ii.

17. Paul Lieberman and Louis Sahagun, *Chicago Tribune*, "Guard troops sweep in; L.A. starting to Quiet," (May 2, 1992) p. 10.

18. Noam Chomsky, *The Culture of Terrorism*.

19. George Jackson, *Blood in My Eye* (Black Classic Press, 1990) p. 7.

20. Kenneth Walsh and Joseph Shapiro, *U.S. News and World Report*, "They are not Our Issues" (May 18, 1992) p. 26.

21. Richard Stevenson, *New York Times*, "Economy Absorbs Another Blow" (May 4, 1992) p. C1-C2.

22. *Ibid.*

23. Walter Williams, *The State Journal-Register*, "Black Leaders Fabricate Hopelessness" (May 7, 1992).

24. Frantz Fanon, *The Wretched of the Earth* (Grove Weidenfeld, 1988) p. 38.

25. Michael Bradley, *The Iceman Inheritence* (Kayode, 1992). Here the author traces the roots of violence in the Western World—as it gains expression in racism and sexism—back to Europe's Ice Age. His theory offers an explanation for the negative influence that Europe has had on the misdevelopment

of the rest of the world. Also see Bradley's forthcoming *Chosen People From the Caucasus: Jewish Origins, Delusions, Deceits and Historical Role in the Slave Trade, Genocide and Cultural Colonization*, where he expounds on his earlier thesis.

26.   Jorge Casuso and Karen Thomas, *Chicago Tribune*, "A Nightmare of Violence in L.A." (May 1, 1992) p. 1 and 4.

27.   Paul Lieberman and Louis Sahagun, *Chicago Sun-Times*, "Guard troops sweep in; L.A. starting to quiet" (May 2, 1992) p. 10.

28.   Acklyn Lynch, *Nightmare Overhanging Darkly: Essays on Black Culture and Resistance*, "Black on Black Homicide" (Third World Press, 1992) C 2.

29.   Janice Hale-Benson, *Black Children: Roots, Culture and Learning Styles* (John Hopkins University Press, 1986) and Amos Wilson, *Black on Black Violence: The Psychodynamics of Black Self-Annihilation in Service of White Domination* (1990).

30.   Kris Parker (KRS-ONE), *Sex and Violence* (album) "Poisonous Products" (1992).

31.   O'Shea Jackson (Ice Cube), *Death Certificate* (album), "A Bird in the Hand" (1992).

32.   Arther Schlesinger, *The Disuniting of America* (W. W. Norton and Co., 1992). Schlesinger vehemently argues in defense of Western Civilization as universal and views multiculturalism as "anti-American." An excellent example of the economic elite's use of the academy as an institution to promote its ideology, culture and values.

33.   Robert Hershey, Jr., *New York Times*, "U.S. Increases Figures Showing Loss of Jobs" (June 4, 1992) p. C2.

34.   Slyvia Nasar, *New York Times*, "Unexplored Territory: A Recession in Services" (February 3, 1991) p. 1.

35.   Madhubuti, p. 59-113.

36.   These programs are dangerous because some Blacks will welcome the police into Black communities, giving up a certain

level of human rights (encouraging repression) as well as civil rights in hopes of detering Black-on-Black violence. Already in Chicago, some middle class as well as poor Blacks have endorsed this.

37. Frantz Fanon, *The Wretched of the Earth*, "Concerning Violence." Also see Amos Wilson's *Black on Black Violence*.

38. George Jackson, *Blood in My Eye*, p. 7.

BAKARI KITWANA is Executive Editor, Third World Press, and General Manager, African American Book Centers in Chicago. He contributed to the essay collection, *Confusion By Any Other Name*. Kitwana holds master's degrees in English and Education from the University of Rochester.

How the L.A. Uprising Will Affect the '92 Election

Stan West

Just a year after President George Bush celebrated his victory over Saddam Hussein, who would have thought that 56 blows to a Black motorist would set the stage for a crushing blow to a Republican regime that once seemed invincible but now garners less than one-third of American support? Few would have guessed the omnipotent White House might topple like a house of cards.

Yet, with just weeks away to that fateful election day, scientific surveys and an informal poll taken by this reporter strongly hint that anger ignited among the electorate since the Los Angeles rebellion could very well translate into voters retiring Bush in favor of Bill Clinton.

Today, in mid-July in middle America, it's hot. Not just the temperature outside, but the heat under the blue and white collars of Americans simmering in this summer of discontent. But to truly grasp the red hot spirit of change sweeping the frustrated American masses, let's return briefly to the scene of the crime.

Sirens soared and fires roared the night justice died. The whole world raged moments after the acquittal of four white

121

cops in the brutal "wilding" of a Black construction worker, emphasizing the dubious role of hate, lies and videotape.

"Few reasonable people will look at that tape of the beating and say there's nothing wrong here," said Ellis Cose, an expert on race relations and editorial page director of the *New York Daily News*. "The point where Black and Hispanic Americans and White Americans part company is that Whites tend to see this as an isolated episode that happened for bizarre reasons in California, whereas Blacks tend to see it as something that's very typical, something that can happen to anybody who is Black and is at the wrong place at the wrong time."

All Americans, especially Blacks, soured at the Simi Valley verdict that let four white cops go for Rodney King's beating. Black Americans also appeared soured with the stagnated Bush regime, so stale that even Black Republicans found it difficult to defend the Bush/Reagan policies that set the stage for what most agree was a racist verdict and an equally racist response to the unrest that followed.

For example, Arthur Fletcher, a Black conservative appointed by Mr. Bush to head the U.S. Commission on Civil Rights, threw his plate against a wall at a fancy Washington eatery when he heard about the verdict. "We're witnessing racial enmity, alienation and despair," he told a *Chicago Tribune* reporter. "This alienation is of such dimensions that it threatens the well-being and security of this nation—unless government acts now!"

Well, by mid-July, the Bush administration had not yet acted in a demonstrative manner, partly on the advice of close advisors who warned that aiding the fundamental causes of disparity and alienation that led to the civil disturbances may be viewed by some whites as rewarding Black rioters.

Will it affect the '92 presidential elections?

"Hell yes," said LA.-based videographer Jeff "Kunta" Callaway in a July 14 telephone interview. Callaway, a former Jerry Brown supporter now pledging his vote to Bill Clinton, said conservative whites he knows in Los Angeles feel "betrayed by Bush because he allowed this racial and economic disparity to get so fuckin' far out of hand...they will vote for anybody but Bush to keep African Americans like me from kicking those Black jockeys down on their manicured lawns before we set their seemingly safe homes ablaze!"

In a series of interviews with more than 500 callers on WVON-AM radio in Chicago, a Black talk show that appeals to middle-class African Americans, ages 25-50, the consensus of the respondents in an informal survey was that Blacks will vote a change in November. Virtually all agreed that what happened in L.A. would effect the voting habits of Blacks, though they differed as to how much and how. Many called for a new Black political movement.

Before Perot dropped out of the race, some felt Texas billionaire H. Ross Perot's undeclared independent campaign was the way to go, especially after Gov. Bill Clinton's attack on rap singer Sister Souljah at Rev. Jesse Jackson's Rainbow Coalition meeting, calling her a "Black racist" and triggering an angry response from Jackson. (On the eve of the Democratic Convention, Jackson gave Clinton a lukewarm endorsement while still making dalliances to Perot.)

Then Perot, in addressing the NAACP in Washington, referred to Blacks as "you people," a gaffe which distanced African Americans already suspicious about the man who said he was against affirmative action. Perot plunged in the polls, and many suspected the comment, among other things, was a factor in his decision to drop out.

Most conceded that even though Clinton was not an ideal choice, there was an "anybody but Bush" push.

Clinton named Senator Al Gore (D-Tenn) his running mate, and the candidate consequently shot up in the polls, beating out Bush and Perot. That two southerners were on the ticket didn't seem to be a problem, even though the liberal wing of the Democratic party—former Gov. Jerry Brown and Rev.

How L.A. Happened

Jesse Jackson—was shut out of the decision-making process. As one elderly African-American woman told this reporter: "So what if white male Southerners are dominating the ticket! I'd vote my dog in office if I thought he could beat Bush. That's all that matters. Bush must go!"

That was the sentiment of hundreds of callers, including young discontents who said they were disillusioned with the process and turned off by the candidates but that they were going to "hold their noses" and vote for Clinton anyway. Even New York Gov. Mario Cuomo admitted he did not agree with Clinton on some issues, such as Clinton's support of the death penalty. He did, however, agree with him more than he did with President Bush.

The same day Cuomo made his statement, President Bush plummeted in a *New York Times*/CBS poll, which showed Clinton gaining in the tight race. On July 13, Clinton actually tied the President when voters were asked how they would vote if the election was held today. The poll showed Bush at 33%, Clinton at 30% and Perot, a dismal 25%. (On the morning of July 16 following the resignation of top aid Ed Rollins, Perot pulled out of the race.) The margin of sampling error of plus or minus three percentage points showed a tie, the lowest rating in history for Bush in any poll.

According to a national survey released July 8, 1992 by Home Box Office and the Joint Center for Political and Economic Studies, the attitudes of Black Americans are of "special interest" in this presidential election year since they represent a substantial share of the voting age population in a number of major states which could determine the outcome of the presidential election. "Their votes are unusually critical this year since the third party candidacy of Texas billionaire H. Ross Perot makes the outcome of the election and the behavior of the electorate very difficult to predict," the study said. Of the presidential hopefuls, Clinton led the field with the support of 43% of those surveyed, followed by Perot with 14% and Bush with 13%. When Perot dropped out, many WVON callers predicted that Clinton would snatch most of his votes, fueling the imaginations of conspiracy theorists.

A major finding of this survey across a wide range of issue areas was a pervasive sense of "dissatisfaction and a desire for change and solutions to problems." This dissatisfaction manifested itself in both liberal and conservative voices.

In the first month after L.A. erupted, CBS pollsters revealed widespread disapproval of the President's domestic policies. One pollster even predicted a change of command in the White House in direct response to the Administration's "mis-handling of urban crises."

In the informal WVON poll taken two days after the rebellion, more than 250 Chicago callers agreed on this one point: the Los Angeles riots would affect the '92 elections. The point where they differed was *how* they would be effected. A few hinted that white backlash might actually help Bush. Many others were waiting to hear what Perot had to say, but more than 200 of them supported Clinton over Bush.

Here's a sampling: one caller named Al, responding to the increasing white backlash theory, predicted widespread conservative white support for even more stringent law and order measures prompted by Willie Hortonesque White House appeals to white fears and the media's repeated coverage of the brutal beating of white trucker Reginald Denny by four Black alleged gang members. Says Al: "I feel this will help George Bush because whites feel that even though you've been stepped on, you shouldn't shout out."

Robert lined up behind Al's analysis. "Bush will be the beneficiary of the post-rebellion period that will galvanize an already suspicious white population that's on the edge of fear and assumes Blacks have a violent nature. No doubt about it, Bush will use this like he used Willie Horton, and it'll work."

The law and order issue should not be discounted because for many white Americans, this issue is intertwined with unspoken fears about Black men. Last year, a University of Chicago study found that 56% of whites believed that Blacks were "prone to violence."

Despite White House appeals to white fear, the issue of incompetence and lack of leadership, the dismal economy and simply a lack in confidence could be the crack in the armor among most of the people interviewed. Ron Brown, the chairman of the Democratic National Committee, predicted the rebellions would cost Mr. Bush the election in November. "Mr. Bush is totally out of touch. Nothing in life experience allies him with the problems of South Central Los Angeles or real people in America."

According to Brown, out of the ashes of hate, Americans who have been spoon-fed a steady diet of Black anger and white fear will seek new leadership to the long-ignored race problem. Times change, and he says, so do voters.

Brown added: "The rebellion will be helpful to the Democrats because the American people will come to realize that the Democrats deal with our nation's problems better than Republicans do, and history has shown us that Republicans just turn a deaf ear. The American people don't trust George Bush, and in November, voters will retire him!"

To see, feel and hear first-hand how Americans were going to respond in the November elections, I travelled by bus from Chicago to Washington with 25 homeless people who felt they could make a difference at the May 16, 1992 "Save Our Children, Save Our Cities" rally held within the shadows of the White House in a park across the street. One of the most poignant quotes came from Randolph Howard, 27, a man who says he is homeless, but not helpless, a man who holds a masters degree in international marketing from Cornell University.

"This is a temporary condition for me, and I realize there's some hope that grassroots leaders will emerge and set a progressive path where others, armed with voter registration cards, will follow. Mr. Bush allowed racism to get out of hand.

How the L.A. Uprising Will Affect the
'92 Election

Now he should pack his bags because he's history," he said flashing his voter card.

Rep. Maxine Waters (D-California) told me backstage at this same event where 250,000 converged to show they could affect meaningful change that the President's own mis-handling of the L.A. rebellion in the spring could be his swan song in the fall. According to Waters: "George Bush doesn't know much about anything. He can't even talk about my idea, enterprise zones, intelligently. They tried to set it up that it was liberals versus conservatives.

"And that's why when Mr. Bush came to Los Angeles and snubbed me and other Democratic leaders, I had to remind them that I was the author of a 1985 resolution calling for enterprise zones. George Bush claimed he wanted to work on both sides of the aisle on the urban agenda problem, yet when he came to my district, he didn't even include me in discussions. He came merely for a photo opportunity."

In an interview on WVON on May 26, Waters said that instead of attacking the problem of rebuilding L.A. and America, "Mr. Bush issued a smoke and mirrors band-aid proposal of warmed-over programs he had already introduced and provided no money. In addition, he's been detrimental to all Americans by not providing a domestic policy. That's why Americans are rising to the occasion and will replace him. I'll help him pack his bags!"

The riots have become a metaphor for everything that's wrong with America. The violent transformation acted out in a dozen U.S. streets and in another dozen foreign capitals symbolizes to many a quiet riot occurring with voters who, for a variety of reasons, are now saying loud and clear the "same old same old" will no longer work.

Few look at Clinton as an ideal choice. But most agree anybody but Bush will do. As the President scrapes the bottom of the barrel in virtually every poll, as racism rages and the economy plummets, Americans of all stripes recognize that the writing is on the White House wall.

Humpty Dumpty is about to take a mighty fall in November.

STAN WEST, former associate editor and foreign correspondent for San Francisco-based Pacific News Services, is the host of the award-winning talk program "World Objective" on WVON-AM Chicago and a columnist for *All Chicago City News*, a bilingual weekly. He is a board member of the Washington, DC-based National Alliance of Third World Journalists. Currently, West is working on a novel on the 500 years of resistance by Blacks, Indians and women since the invasion of Christopher Columbus.

Rebellion In Los Angeles: The Crises of Racism and Capitalism

Ron Daniels

> Our cities are crime-haunted dying grounds. Huge sectors of our youth—and countless others—face permanent unemployment. Those of us who are able to work find our paychecks able to purchase less and less. Neither the courts nor the prisons contribute anything resembling justice or reformation. The schools are unable—or unwilling—to educate our children for the real world of our struggles. Meanwhile, the officially approved epidemic of drugs threatens to wipe out the minds of our best young warriors.
>
> Economic, cultural, and spiritual depression stalk Black America, and the price for survival often appears to be more than we are able to pay. On every side, in every area of our lives, the American institutions in which we have placed our trust are unable to cope with the crises they have created by their single-minded dedication to profits for some and white supremacy above all.

As Dr. Maulana Karenga constantly reminds, it is imperative that we maintain "historical memory." The above analysis comes from the Preamble to the National Black Political Agenda adopted at the historic Gary Black Political Convention 20 years ago. The insurrection/rebellion which exploded in South Central Los Angeles is a brutal reminder that "the more things change, the more they stay the same."

The verdict in the Rodney King police beating trial

129

reaffirmed for the world what Africans in America already know. Racism is alive and well in the U.S. Like the Dred Scott Decision in 1857, the verdict in the King case proclaimed loudly and clearly that Black people have no rights which a racist and exploitive system is compelled to respect. The rage that erupted into violent rebellion and a massive groundswell of grassroots protest across the country signalled that Black poor and working people—the masses—are "sick and tired of being sick and tired." Hence, the battle cry which reverberated throughout this nation and the world was, "no justice, no peace."

For nearly 25 years, racism—and its continuing impact on the aspirations of Black America—has not been a major priority on the public policy agenda. Once the walls of southern apartheid crumbled under the relentless onslaught of the Civil Rights Revolution of the '60s, white America grew weary of the movement. With the removal of the "white only" signs from water fountains, restrooms, lunch counters, beaches and other public accommodations and conveyances, and with the passage of various civil rights laws and statutes in the '50s and '60s, the perception in much of white America was that these strides towards freedom were sufficient. White America had given enough.

But the rebellions in Watts, Newark, Detroit, Washington, DC and scores of other urban ghettos in the mid to late '60s sent a warning that the passage of a few laws and the eradication of the most visible indignities were not sufficient. There was the crucial matter of economic equity and parity for a people whose free labor helped to build this nation, a people whose free labor has never been rewarded with reparations or a substantial endowment or stake to undergird their status as "emancipated" African "citizens." These questions of equity and parity were raised by Martin Luther King just before he was felled by an assassin's bullet in Memphis in 1968.

The Kerner Commission, which studied the rebellions of

the '60s, including the violent reaction to King's assassination, concluded, in essence, that there were two Americas, one white, one Black, separate and unequal. The cold fact is that in 1992, for the masses of Black people, virtually nothing has changed since 1968. The Kerner Commission Report did very little to keep racism and the plight of the Black poor at the top of the American Agenda.

Indeed, we should recall that in 1968 Richard Nixon was swept into the presidency on a wave of "white backlash" and the call to "law and order." Nixon began the process of curtailing civil rights enforcement and slowing down Black advancement through a calculated policy of "benign neglect." Jimmy Carter, who succeeded Gerald Ford in wake of Nixon's fall from grace, essentially told Black America to downplay Black issues and Black concerns. In the face of the declining popularity of the Black Agenda, the word from Jimmy Carter to Black America was "trust me." Race relations and the plight of Black people had also fallen from white America's grace.

Ronald Reagan was not interested in gaining the trust of Black America. The Reagan agenda was clear: promote and exploit racial fears and antagonisms as a means of advancing the interests of the rich and the super-rich. Ronald Reagan unapologetically launched an era of race politics designed to split off a substantial number of white middle-class and working-class voters from the Democratic Party. He suggested that Black gains via civil rights, affirmative action and social programs were "burdens" on the backs of white people. Black people were gaining at the expense of white people, and of course that was not fair. Politically motivated racism was promoted and legitimized from the highest office in the land.

The strategy worked. Large numbers of white voters did indeed abandon the Democratic Party to become "Reagan Democrats." To their discredit, however, the National Democratic Party not only retreated from its commitment to civil rights and affirmative action, but the Democrats, who were a majority in both the House of Representatives and the Senate, voted the "Reagan Revolution" into law. The revolution virtually destroyed social and economic support programs for poor and working people and drastically reduced federal aid to the urban centers. The revolution simultaneously increased military/war spending while providing gaping tax loopholes for the wealthy. The revolution further enriched and entrenched the rich and the super-rich in their positions of power and privilege in U.S. society.

By 1988 leaders like Governor Bill Clinton (the wannabe president) from the moderate-conservative Democratic Leadership Conference were vigorously urging the Democratic Party to become more "Reaganesque" in order to win the presidency. Jesse Jackson as a candidate for President was ridiculed and shunned for being too liberal on racial issues and social-economic policy. In essence, the moderate-conservative forces within the Democratic Party were saying that the way to win back the Reagan Democrats and recapture the White House was by downplaying racism and the crisis in the ghettos and barrios of urban America. Hence, both the Republicans and Democrats must share the blame for deprioritizing racism, race relations and the urban crisis in the U.S. Both establishment parties are responsible for fostering and overlooking the injustices which spawned the explosion in South Central Los Angeles.

For nearly 25 years the interests, issues and agendas of the masses of Black people, minorities and poor and working people in the inner cities have been abandoned and neglected by the U.S. government. Black people and the oppressed have been left to "suffer peacefully." Now the bitter harvest of racism, abandonment and neglect has come to fruition. The root causes of the rebellion in Los Angeles, however, are far deeper than the flawed governmental policies and the racial politics to which the establishment parties have succumbed over the last two decades.

The Crises of Racism and Capitalism

The rebellion in Los Angeles should cause Blacks to reflect on what the Black Nation proclaimed at the historic Black Political Convention in Gary some 20 years ago. "The crises we face as Black people are the crises of the entire society. They go deep to the very bones and marrow, to the essential nature of America's economic, political and cultural systems. They are the natural end-product of a society built on the twin foundations of...racism and ...capitalism." This fundamental reality has not changed. White supremacy is still the "order."

The rebellion also unmasked another crisis we face as Black people, and that is the crisis of Black leadership, a political leadership which has gained access to the system but largely has been co-opted, neutralized and rendered ineffective by their uncritical participation in and/or slavish devotion to the system. Black leadership suffers from amnesia when it comes to remembering the political axioms uttered at Gary: "...all truly Black politics must begin with this truth: *The American system does not work for the masses of our people, and it cannot be made to work without radical fundamental change.*" Unfortunately, far from offering a vision of radical change, many Black leaders have become apologists for the system which oppresses our people.

In spite of this weak leadership, the masses of Black people and the oppressed have spoken in the streets of South Central Los Angeles and in more than 30 cities across this nation. Their verdict is—"no justice no peace." In the critical period ahead, a visionary and committed leadership must emerge. That leadership must emerge from among the activists, community-based leaders, intellectuals and scholars who are on the frontlines of the struggle with the masses of our people on a day-to-day basis. It must be the charge if this new political leadership is to stand firm on the principle that there are certain "inalienable rights" which must not be violated by any government. This leadership must refuse, in principle, to apologize for

133

the rebellion in Los Angeles. This leadership must recognize the insurrection in Los Angeles as a rebellion against racism, massive inequality, neglect, abuse and the tyranny of the rich and the super-rich—a rebellion against a system of white supremacy.

In the spirit of Malcolm, a new leadership must rise which will continue the rebellion/insurrection at the ballot box and in the streets, a leadership which will hear the voices of those who gathered at Gary demanding that Black leadership and Black politics accept the "challenge to consolidate and organize our own Black role as the vanguard in the struggle for a new society...The society we seek cannot come unless Black people organize to advance its coming."

A racist, exploitive, capitalist society is responsible for the rebellion that rocked Los Angeles, America and the world. The ancestors' exhortation is to be self-reliant, to take seriously the task of building viable, African-centered cultural, educational, economic and political institutions, to be uncompromising in our revolutionary commitment in breaking the chains of white supremacy and white domination over the lives of our people and the lives of the oppressed. Out of the ruin and catastrophe wrought on our people and the world by a decadent and dying "civilization," our challenge is to shape a new African people. Out of the fire and ashes of rebellion, African people must forge a new people, a new nation and a new world order.

RON DANIELS is an independent candidate in the 1992 campaign for President of the United States. In 1988, Daniels was the Southern Regional Coordinator and Deputy Campaign Manager for the 1988 Jesse Jackson for President Campaign. He also served as the Executive Director, National Rainbow Coalition in 1987, and the National Co-Chair, National Black Independent Political Party, 1980-1985.

part three . . .

MEDIA: NO MELODY OR ANALYSIS

America's poem, or,

81 seconds and 56 blows

Mwatabu S. Okantah

we saw them
beat him.
they beat him, and they beat him,
and they beat him,
they beat
him;
81 seconds and
56 blows.

they were tried
by a jury of their peers.
Lady Justice is not
blind.
she has been
blindfolded.
no justice.
no peace.
America's black
whitemare raging
once again in the streets:

you say
you just don't understand.
you say
we look dangerous
to you.
you pretend
you don't know why
we are so angry.
you try so hard not to remember,
you depend on us
to live and
forget:

it
began
sometime during the fifteenth
century.
first the Portuguese,
and then the Spanish, and then
the Dutch, and then
the French,
and then the English,
and then the
Americans
raided
in Africa.

no African holocaust memorials
in Europe
or America today,
only the slave relics house in Badagri,
only cells on Goree Island,
only dungeons
at Christianborg, Elmina

Why L.A. Happened

and Cape Coast Castles
to remind us
the price
paid
for the second class
citizenship of an
exslave.

you say
you just don't understand.
living in ghettoes
reminds us everyday of those things
you so easily forget.
when descendents of rape
victims live
in the house of their
  fathers,
they
sleep with the enemy.
they suffer
the enemy
in themselves.

this is not the 1960s.
no Malcolm
to tell us the dream is nightmare.
even Martin said
your freedom check has been
returned,
stamped
"Insufficient Funds."
another generation
is burning
and the nation
is bankrupt

America's poem, or, 81 seconds and 56 blows

today:

you say
you just don't understand.
we live in your house.
we are strangers.
we see you in the workplace.
we are invisible.
we die in your wars.
we kill for you.
we make you laugh.
we sing, we dance for you.
you do not see us.
you see us
only when we wreak havoc
in your streets,
framed nightly on your tv screens,
you see us only
when we leap
out of your wildest dreams.

we saw them beat him.
you say
you just don't understand.
you have eyes.
you refuse to see.
to see us,
you have to look into our lives,
into that darkening
  terror
mirror reflecting
your deeply
deep felt
why:

Why L.A. Happened

you don't understand.
you live in fear.
you have not
  listened.
you
turned
a deaf ear . . .

MWATABU S. OKANTAH is a poet, lecturer and performance artist who has performed in universities and cultural events across the globe, including Cheikh Anta Diop University, Dakar, Senegal; the 12th Annual Meeting of the American Culture Association in Toronto, Canada; the 20th Annual Conference of the African Heritage Studies Association in Washington, DC; and the 13th Annual Third World Conference in Chicago, Illinois. A critically acclaimed poet, Okantah was named Rotary International Group Study Exchange Fellow to Nigeria in 1989 and New Jersey State Council on the Arts Poetry Fellow in 1980. His poetry and articles have appeared in the *Village Voice*, *Essence*, the *Final Call*, *Reggae Report* and the *Cleveland Plain Dealer*. He is co-editor of *Hell is for Those Who Glitter* (1978) and author of *To Sing A Dark Song* (1977).

The Los Angeles Rebellion:
Class, Race and Misinformation

Charles E. Simmons

Now that the smoke has cleared and the ashes and rubble
have been swept away across the various communities of this
'City of Angels'—South Central, Downtown, Korea Town,
Pico and Hollywood—the debates and confrontations have
turned to reconstruction. African-American construction con-
tractors, asserting a new militancy, shut down building sites
from which they were excluded. Immigrant workers have gone
on strike for higher wages and a union in this historically anti-
union town. The Crips and the Bloods youth gangs, who have
been shooting each other and passersby for more than a decade,
called for and have maintained a truce, despite opposition from
police.

Some Los Angeles area residents have focused their
attention on the media which gave voice to much election-year
posturing; conservative local and national candidates and other
establishment bosses denounced the angry commentary of
frontline rappers, Sister Souljah and Ice-T. These artists speak
for the many Black, Latino, Asian and Anglo youth who daily
endure the hostility of California's militarized police forces.

141

Why L.A. Happened

They speak for the youth's parents and grandparents who have become fixtures in the growing unemployment lines in Tinsel Town's valley of sun and fun. (*NO SELLOUT*, 20)

Headlines and commentaries, such as "Blacks Revolt In Los Angeles," did not completely summarize the explosive events of April 30 through May 5—symbolic of the U.S. media's incomprehensive portrayal of issues involving race and class. While it is true that a large segment of the Los Angeles-area African-American community revolted, they were not alone. They were joined by at least an equivalent number of persons of Latin American descent, many white youth from Hollywood and a smaller number of Asian Americans. Many homeless families and Vietnam veterans also protested the Simi Valley court decision to acquit members of the Los Angeles Police Department (LAPD) charged simply with the use of excessive force against Black motorist, Rodney King.

According to police records, 42% of the participants in the rebellion were African American, 44% Latino, 9% white and 2% other. Also significant is that around the time of the 1965 Watts Rebellion, that community was more than 70% African American. The decrease in the upwardly mobile Black population in Watts and South Central and its expansion into other Los Angeles communities went officially unnoticed by the media—perhaps because in general, poor areas are only covered during a crisis. Demographics are needed to accurately assess the present social crisis, yet mainstream editors and news anchors insisted on portraying L.A. gangs as exclusively Black or Latino. In reality, they reflect the racial and economic composition of the neighborhoods. Furthermore, the various communities are internally stratified; racial identification signs posted on the windows and doors of some businesses did not guarantee protection as during the rebellions of the 1960s.

Although there is friction between Black consumers and Korean merchants, this issue was overstated by the media. The Los Angeles problem has much deeper historical and social roots. As Elaine H. Kim, Korean-American professor of Asian American Studies at the University of California-Berkeley, explained in *Newsweek* (5/18/92),

> My consciousness was shaped by the civil rights movement led by African Americans, who taught me to reject the false choice between being treated as a perpetual foreigner and relinquishing my own identity for someone else' Anglo-American one...the so-called Black-Korean problem is a decontextualized manifestation of a much larger problem. The roots lie not in the Korean immigrant-owned corner store situated in a community ravaged by poverty and police violence, but stretch far back to the corridors of corporate and government offices in Los Angeles, Sacramento, and Washington D.C.

There are at least four reasons for this consistently distorted reportage, much of which was discussed in great detail 20 years ago in the U.S. government studies on the causes of the '60s rebellions (Kerner Report) and by media scholars, but most of it was forgotten after the smoke cleared (Bagdikian, 127; Parenti, 156).

1. The media overwhelmingly fail to incorporate sufficient information about the social context or historical development of issues involving race and class.
2. Too few media professionals and managers are people of color.
3. Crisis reporting dominates the coverage of Black, Brown, poor and blue-collar white communities, resulting in consistent misinformation.
4. The increasing monopolization of media ownership discourages in-depth reporting of certain controversial issues which may offend suburban-based advertisers, more affluent consumers and the owners themselves.

Why L.A. Happened

CLASS, RACE AND MISINFORMATION

To place the rebellion in an appropriate historical context (something the media failed to do), it should be pointed out that during the past decade, the Department of Justice has received more than 47,000 police brutality complaints, which triggered major investigations by the agency and by U.S. Congressman John Conyers, Jr. (D-Mich), Chair of the House Judiciary Subcommittee on Criminal Justice. Students of police brutality should read the horrors revealed in the Subcommittee's reports going back to 1983. (U.S. Congress) Less than 200 of those complaints have resulted in fines or prosecution against the police. In Los Angeles, thousands of brutality complaints are filed each month, but only a few result in penalties because investigations and decisions are made by the police officers themselves. (Christopher)

Two years prior to the beating of Rodney King, an African-American police officer, Donald Jackson, complained publicly about the use of excessive force by Southern California suburban police. Jackson was joined by a Black female officer in a statement alleging that pro-nazi and Klan literature were regularly circulated within the police stations and placed on the officers' cars. Then Jackson himself became a victim when in Long Beach, white police cursed him and smashed his head through a large store window, all of which was taped by a camera crew and aired on national television the next day. At the subsequent hearing and trial, the accused police claimed that Jackson had thrown himself through the window as a tactic to make the white officers look bad. They were acquitted.

In 1991, in the largely Black and Latino Watts district of Los Angeles, two brothers of Samoan descent were apprehended in front of their home by a multi-racial pair of police. Reloading their weapons twice, the police shot the men 19 times. In court, the police pled self-defense. The case ended in a 'hung' (inconclusive) decision by the jury. As of this writing, it has not been decided whether or not there will be a new trial. (The fact that some of the police accused of excessive force are not always white demands that we focus our attention on the *system itself* and how it impacts negatively on the broad classes and races of people.)

In Milwaukee, Wisconsin and Boston, Massachusetts, white men accused Black men of killing their wives, and in both cases, the media hurriedly published stories about the behavior of savage animals and such. In both cases, the white men were eventually charged with murder. However, the damage had been done; Blacks had been severely castigated throughout the local and national media continuously for several months. This caused the community extreme anger about the media's irresponsibility which severely damaged the Black image.

In New York City, a 21 year-old Puerto Rican man discovered asleep in a stolen vehicle, according to witnesses, was beaten to death by city police. Black and Puerto Rican community critics sharply complained that the District Attorney cooperated with the police in the trial which resulted in their acquittal. Community residents condemned the police chief, the Mayor of New York City (both African Americans) and the entire criminal justice system. They demanded better organizational policy, police discipline and community control.

In a widely publicized case in 1991, a Korean merchant fatally shot a Black teenage girl in a dispute over the price of a bottled soft drink. The merchant was convicted but given a suspended sentence, with no imprisonment. The judge, a white woman, was supported by an appellate court and many of the local bar associations. Following a year of continuous Black and Latino community protest, including a petition to remove her, the judge was re-elected by an overwhelming majority of the voters.

Such consistently unfair verdicts in the 1990s, along with the media's superficial reporting, have promoted the view stated in the 1857 Dred Scott Supreme Court decision, that

Why L.A. Happened

Black people have no rights that white people are bound to respect.

Numerous young white males have also complained about the excessive use of force against *them* by the California police. In 1990, a locally aired videotape showed police choking a white youth until he fell unconscious. That police action was in response to a complaint by neighbors of a noisy party. Although reporters dodged the issue, the incident is symbolic of why many white youth joined the "Rodney King" rebellion.

In addition to not providing the proper historical context of police brutality to the King beating, the media appear unable to distinguish between race and class issues—e.g., the white working poor or the decrease in real income among the middle classes. A broad segment of white America—particularly those in the major urban communities, the small farmers, Vietnam veterans, single mothers and children and numerous senior citizens—now experience conditions similar to many Blacks and Latinos, e.g., lack of jobs, inadequate social services, indecent housing, inferior education and poor health care. The findings from such an analysis would contradict the traditional theories, i.e., that jobs are plentiful, that all jobs are sufficient for a decent living—the problem is with the poor colored people who would rather complain and antagonize the police than work.

These developments coincide with the economic decline of the U.S. in the past two decades and the exit of jobs from the U.S. manufacturing sector to the Third World source of cheap labor. Although it is still true that 7-15% of Black adults and 50% or more of Black youth are unemployed, the largest percentage of the 40 million Americans who live below the official poverty line are white women and children; the largest number of Americans on welfare is also white. The media consistently neglect to report these facts of American life.

Governmental budget cuts have also contributed to poverty. The national housing budget has been cut by more than half in the past decade. Consequently, many working Americans cannot afford housing. (Parenti, Harrington) Health care has faced sweeping cuts across the board, affecting young and old. Infant mortality in American cities places the U.S. between 17-22 internationally, which is a poorer rating than some developing nations in Africa and Asia.

Among the urban homeless, which includes all racial groups, the numbers range from the tens and hundreds of thousands in Los Angeles to some three million persons nationwide. These figures are most difficult to verify because homeless people often go uncounted by the census. In addition, the lack of a permanent residential address makes government assistance unobtainable. Nor are the homeless allowed to vote in many municipalities. Thus, many individuals are virtually invisible to the government with no personal records to speak of. Some of the homeless live in their automobiles, some are veterans, some are mental patients released due to the cuts in health care, some live on college campuses, but most are children of all races.

According to Earl Ofari Hutchinson, author of the *Mugging of Black America*, among those arrested and incarcerated annually, the largest numbers are Black, Latino and young males *of all races*. In fact, not only does the U.S. have the largest prison population in the world, there are four times as many Black inmates in U.S. prisons than there are in South Africa.

Rampant criminal activity has motivated many private American citizens of all social categories to arm themselves with various weaponry. The annual murder rate for Los Angeles exceeds 400 fatalities, and most of those are perpetrated by people who know one another—many cases involve family members. In addition, most assaults occur within the same racial and ethnic groups, i.e., white-on-white, Latino-on-Latino or Black-on-Black. (McFate, Ofari)

Why L.A. Happened

Records dating back to the early 1700s show a long history of riots and uprisings over issues of labor, agricultural policies, suffrage, war and peace, veterans benefits and assorted political issues. (Headley, Mazon) Yet, the media emphasize Black males, through the frequent use of negative descriptions and photographs, as violence-prone, a threat to white residents whose real threat are the unemployed white youth in their own communities.

RACIAL DIVERSITY AMONG
MEDIA PROFESSIONALS

Black and Brown media employees who gather and comment on the news comprise 9% of professionals, up from 1% in the 1960s. Among management in both broadcasting and print media where the decisions of what to publish are made, there are less than 2%. Consider that statistic in light of the fact that people of color constitute about one-fourth of the overall U.S. population and are actually majorities in such cities as Los Angeles and other large urban areas. Again, this problem of underrepresentation was identified and criticized loudly in the 1967 government study of the 120 rebellions of the 1960s. (Kerner)

Although the Black and Brown middle classes have substantially expanded, there has been a much larger and broader expansion of the working poor and unemployed poor in the two groups. (Hutchinson) Few middle-class reporters or newscasters of any race have sufficient contact with or know much about the poorer central urban areas unless there is a crisis. The ignorance of reporters regarding demographic shifts, along with the current patterns of advertising and news coverage which caters to the more affluent and predominantly white suburban communities, have combined to create a devastating psychological climate for all. (Bagdikian)

This came across frequently in on-the-spot newscasts of

the Los Angeles rebellion. Reporters seldom identified the accurate locations of the various inner-city communities and expressed shock at the hostile attitudes of many residents toward media employees and police. They did not realize that many urban residents identify the media with local government authorities and police, none of which are as positively perceived in the urban communities as in the suburbs. To some degree the police are viewed in the affluent communities as protectors and neighbors, but in the poorer central urban areas where police regularly blockade the streets, conduct door-to-door searches for suspects and fly overhead continuously in military-style helicopters with spotlights flashing, they are perceived as another major problem. Or, as many urban youth say frequently, the police are just another gang with bigger and better equipment.

CRISIS REPORTING

Media coverage of events in urban areas tends to focus on crime from a police and suburban perspective; seldom are those reports balanced with the viewpoints of the impacted community. The police focus on the criminal as the beginning and end of the issue; community voices emphasize the social and economic factors. In addition, Black people across the U.S. often say that an African American will only appear on the front (or obituary) page of a daily newspaper or prominently on the broadcast news as the result of their criminal activity or athletic performance. Having been an assistant to a Black member of the U.S. House of Representatives (John Conyers, Jr.), this writer can argue from experience how difficult it is to interest the press on issues other than the negative experiences of the Black community.

For example, media coverage of the Los Angeles rebellion generally focused on the early allegation that some 6,000 fires had been set by gangs of Black and Brown arsonists. Actually, that figure reflected the number of calls made to the fire departments, not the number of fires. In addition, most fires elicited multiple calls. But the reporters didn't corroborate the information. Later, some reports emerged from police and residents that some fires had been set by the owners of the buildings who were seeking to obtain insurance money. The official number of fires was later reduced to about 600.

The media also promoted the idea that Black and Brown gang members were responsible for the violence which resulted in about 51 fatalities primarily of Black and Brown people. Yet, there were no autopsies and few witnesses to establish the circumstances of most of the deaths, including six Black and Brown young men who were shot in the head assassination style. However, one small paragraph in the *Los Angeles Times* (6/11/92) conceded that "according to logs from the city's Emergency Command Center...a 'highly organized' group of white men and women were downtown on the riot's first night, working under a leader who timed their actions, giving them 'so many seconds to break windows with dumbbells and...initiate incendiary devices.'"

MEDIA MONOPOLIES: TRENDS

Although racism and elitism have existed in the media long before this era of global corporate domination, media organizations are more profit-oriented than ever, requiring them to concentrate almost exclusively on wealthy advertisers and upscale clients who live in almost total isolation from the working classes and people of color in the inner cities.

These new robber barons represent the largest single sector of the U.S. empire. The communication industry giants now own or control newspapers, magazines, radio and television broadcasting, book publishing, entertainment and tele-communications. According to Prof. Ben Bagdikian in the *Media Monopoly*, some 27 corporate giants own more than 85% of all U.S. and much international media; the trend is toward increasing consolidation, which produces a decreasing amount of hard and in-depth news and information, and more fluff. Can anyone really expect controversial coverage of General Motors, Gulf Oil or other such corporations when they own the news organization?

If the increased monopolization of the media is a trend, and it seems to be, the public should expect little improvement from mainstream sources. More reliance must be placed upon those daring alternative organs, such as the *Final Call* (a fine successor to *Muhammad Speaks*), the *Guardian*, the *Progressive*, the *Nation* and *Liberation News*, which have published honestly during the past 20 to 40 years. The list should also include *Mother Jones* magazine, *In These Times, Sojourner* and the *New York City Sun* (perhaps the most fearless among the African-American weeklies in the tradition of the abolitionists). Also read *Essence* and the relatively new *Emerge*; and listen to Pacifica Radio which is aired in New York City, Washington, DC, Los Angeles and San Francisco. If these stations are unavailable in your area, then organize a media watch committee within your existing religious, community or social organizations to subscribe to C-Span and the periodicals mentioned.

To be watched is the new movement in low-powered underground community radio. These activists have asserted their right to participate in the airwaves which, according to the Federal Communication Commission, belong to the public. Another newcomer is the serious youth-oriented entertainment publication *NO SELLOUT*, which includes strong doses of African-American history. This rap/hip hop magazine is published in Inglewood, California by young African Americans. Their July 1992 edition carried an extensive interview with Sister Souljah and discussions about positive and negative aspects of the liberation lyrics. This politically conscious sector of the new Black music has placed the establishment —from George Bush down to the local sheriffs—on a collision course with the First Amendment's guarantee of the freedom of expression. The artists have been identified by the power structure as the Malcolm X's of music and are dangerous to those who run the nation because the new Black music of rebellion appeals to youth of all races and nations.

The immediate concern of the media today should be to evaluate their coverage of the rebellion and provide follow-up articles and seminars to tell the truth to themselves and the public. The media workers must study the difficult issues of class and race and the historical context in which they operate.

And will the mainstream daily media dare to focus on government-sanctioned violence against society? Now that the cold war has left many intelligence agents with little to do on the international front, the government appears to be emphasizing the use of the FBI and other government gangs to resolve the domestic youth problems. According to numerous publications and government reports about the FBI/CIA project, COINTELPRO, set up to disrupt civil and human rights organizations during the 1960s and 1970s, the 'dirty tricks' used abroad—including drug trafficking (McCoy, Churchill) and assassinations—were brought home and applied to U.S. domestic organizations and individuals, especially in California where the focus was on the Black Panthers, US and Chicano activists. (Acuna, 259) Professor and veteran human rights activist, Angela Davis, raised the question two years ago in her speech to the annual convention of the National Lawyers Guild in Los Angeles: Is it any wonder that "Black youth in California now refer to the CIA as the Cocaine Importing Agency?" However, except for those government employees officially charged with misconduct, the mainstream daily media seldom report on this activity. This writer attended the U.S. Congressional hearings on Contragate in 1986 when presidential advisor to Ronald Reagan, Oliver North, was being discussed. When the question arose about the participation of secret government agencies raising money by drug dealing, the committee closed the hearings to the public and the media acted as if nothing had happened.

Community leaders in South Central, including some ministers, asked whether those same disruptive tactics may be hidden within the drive-by shootings and inter-gang confrontations at a time when youth gangbangers have expressed the desire for a truce. Numerous youth have reported that police frequently apprehend a suspected gang member, drive him to a distant and hostile community, then throw him into the hands of rival gang members with full knowledge of the result. Yet, mainstream media has not discussed this issue. (Rhambo)

There are a minority of honorable individual journalists in practically every city who toil within the mainstream media, who go wherever necessary to search for truth and have the courage to tell it—and they are to be commended. Among the best is the noted and fearless columnist Peggy Peterman at the *St. Petersburg Times* in Florida. She was presented the prestigious Ida B. Wells Award several years ago by the National Association of Black Journalists (NABJ) for her distinguished work in the St. Petersburg area. In Los Angeles, a group of courageous young reporters and editors work at the *Los Angeles Times* and other news organizations, such as editor Angela Clayton. They are a lonely group fighting an uphill battle from within, and the community should support them at every opportunity. Most reporters don't make policy and can't guarantee that what they write will actually appear without revision of content by editors who are often older and probably more biased. There are only a tiny percentage of persons of color in management, less in the ownership sector. For what is important here is not only the character of a minority of journalists, but also the overall character and goals of those who own the media corporations.

The much-publicized posters on the Los Angeles streets, "NO JUSTICE, NO PEACE," was a fundamental human rights demand that has been made throughout U.S. history and around the world by movements for social and economic justice. Two years ago, the African National Congress of South Africa/ Azania concretized that slogan by incorporating the United Nations' Universal Declaration of Human Rights into its constitution which seeks to guide the direction of a new South Africa into the 21st century. A major difference between the U.S. Constitution and the 45-year old UDHR is that the latter is more specific and includes guarantees of economic rights to employment, housing, education, health care and unemployment benefits for everyone; the American document merely refers to the much too vague "Life, Liberty and the Pursuit of Happiness."

The embattled world has a right and a need to know the truth about its human rights conditions, reasons and goals from all sides of the issues, including the views of the have-nots from Southern California and Haiti to South Africa, and reliable news from the mainstream media would be most welcome. But information consumers who desire the truth right now had better rush out and purchase alternative sources, compare the two, and then make up their own minds.

SOURCES

1. *NO SELLOUT:* Black Rap Magazine, pg. 20; 4 July 92, Inglewood, CA.
2. *The Report of the National Advisory Commission on Civil Disorders* (The Kerner Report). New York: Bantam Books, 1968. See page 362. Also, *The Media Monopoly*, Ben Bagdikian. Boston: Beacon Press, 1990. Also, *Make-Believe Media*, Michael Parenti. New York: St. Martins Press, 1992.
3. Hutchinson, Earl Ofari, *The Mugging of Black America*. Chicago: African American Images, 1990.
4. The Warren Christopher Report on the Los Angeles Police Department (Los Angeles City Council), 1992.
5. Hutchinson, op. cit., pgs. 17 and 32.

6. Parenti, Michael, *Democracy for the Few.* New York: St. Martins Press, 1988. Also see *The New American Poverty*, Michael Harrington. New York: Penguin Books, 1984.

7. Headley, Joel Tyler, *The Great Riots of New York: 1712-1875.* New York: Dover Press, 1971. Also, *The Zoot Suit Riots*, Mauricio Mazon. Austin: University of Texas Press, 1984. Also, *Ghetto Revolts*, Joe R. Feagan and Harlan Hahn. New York: McMillan, 1973.

8. McFate, Katherine, *Black Crime, White Fear.* Washington, DC: The Joint Center for Political and Economic Studies, 1992.

9. Hamilton, Cynthia, *Apartheid in an American City: The Case of the Black Community in Los Angeles.* Van Nuys: Labor/Community Strategy Center, 1989.

10. McCoy, Alfred, *The Politics of Heroin in Southeast Asia.* New York: Harper Colophon Books, 1973. Also, *Agents of Repression: The FBI's Secret Wars Against the Black Panther Party and the American Indian Movement*, Ward Churchill and Jim Vander Wall. Boston: South End Press, 1988. Also, *Occupied America: A History of Chicanos, Rodolfo Acuna.* New York: Harper & Row, 1988.

11. Interview with Tim Rhambo, Day One community worker and former gang member, at a forum held at the Black and Latino Book Store in Pasadena, CA, July 20, 1992.

12. "A Bill of Rights for a New South Africa" (ANC of Azania Constitutional Committee, Johannesburg, South Africa), 1990.

13. *The Selected Writings of W.E.B. DuBois*, ed. Walter Wilson. New York: Mentor Books, 1970, pg. 354.

CHARLES E. SIMMONS, J.D. teaches journalism and law at California State University-Los Angeles. He holds an M.S. from Columbia University and a Juris Doctor from Georgetown. Simmons was a United Nations correspondent for *Muhammad Speaks*, and his articles have appeared in *U.S.A. Today*, the *Detroit News*, the *St. Petersburg Times*, the *Washington Afro American*, the Associated Press and *Africa Asia.* Simmons also served on the staff of U.S. Congressman, John Conyers, Jr.

What Los Angeles Means:
"Negroes Are Lynched in America"

William M. Mandel

Izvestia, the second largest paper in Russia, is hysterically anti-Communist. Yet, even its U.S. correspondent recognized the events in Los Angeles following the acquittal of the four police officers for what they were: "The events of the past few days in Los Angeles, the 'city of angels,' confirmed that which our political figures and world-affairs commentators had said for long years and which our readers and listeners had long ceased to believe: Negroes are lynched in America." (May 4)

As far as the author has been able to determine, no American TV or radio network or station (including liberal Pacifica), no newspaper had the perceptivity to draw that conclusion. However, *Comic Buyers Guide*, the trade weekly of the comic book industry, did run a paid ad by Eclipse Books (publisher of political issues trading cards) on May 1 which said:

> Notably absent from the carnage toll were any accounts as to who had been killed, or by whom. The listener knowledgeable about how events are packaged into 'stories' soon became aware that a familiar tight-rope act was being performed beneath the facade of assiduous

Why L.A. Happened

news-gathering...*Because many were killed by a police department already charged and acquitted of using brutality, the manner of their demise was not mentioned.* (author's emphasis)

We now know that of the 51 deaths, 41 were by gunshot wounds. All were civilians—not one cop, sheriff's deputy or National Guardsman, despite the alleged shout of "it's Uzi time" publicized by Ted Koppel, among others. In addition, 198 of the injured were hit by bullets. Yet, even a police spokesman said that the number of incidents of gunfire aimed at officers was only "20 or 30." Three cops were actually hit out of the total of 239 shooting victims. Although there were a couple of cases of white civilians killing African Americans and a near equal number of the opposite, the extraordinary up-close TV coverage showed only two instances of gunfire: (1) a white civilian on a roof carefully taking aim and shooting a long gun (rifle or shotgun) repeatedly at unseen people below, a clip never shown after the first day, and (2) Korean shopkeepers shooting pistols without taking cover, which implied that they were not in danger.

Despite these statistics assembled from various issues of the *Los Angeles Times*, *not one picture of a policeman using a gun was carried by TV*, although on May 2, the *L.A. Times* admitted that 11 people had been killed by law enforcement officers. That the numbers were being managed for publication is clear from the fact that on the next day, the *New York Times* put the number at seven, according to "the local authorities," *four less than the day before*, despite the fact that total reported dead had risen to 44 from 40 the previous day. And on May 24, the *L.A. Times* made it 10.

What one had in Los Angeles was a massacre by the police, set free to do this by the acquittal in Simi Valley. Inasmuch as this massacre was aimed overwhelmingly at minorities (26 Black, 18 Latino dead), in the American historical context, this was lynch justice against Blacks, and Yankee imperialism against Latinos. The use of deadly force by police is justified when necessary to protect oneself, a fellow officer or a civilian from deadly force. But the numbers—20 or 30 cops shot *at* versus 236 civilians actually shot (plus three police)—make it clear that the overwhelming majority of killings and woundings by the police was not in defense of themselves or anyone else.

This was lynch law. No authorization of "shoot to kill" to stop the looting or to discourage curfew violations was issued. No one has informed us how many of the persons killed were armed, how many were shot in the back (some admittedly were), what they were actually doing when shot nor of how the bullets extracted from their bodies compare to bullets used in police guns. In the 10 instances in which killing was acknowledged to have been by police or sheriff's deputies (one) or National Guard (one), the police versions have been specifically contradicted by civilian witnesses in all but two cases, and in one of those the man killed was unarmed and not the one who actually was pointing a gun. Six of those 10 were African American, four Latino. They left 20 children, with four on the way. *Guns were recovered from only two of the victims.*

The purpose of assembling this data and advancing this reasoning is not simply to express outrage. It is to provide material with which to reverse the impression that the media have sought to create upon public opinion: of a poor, downtrodden police force hesitant to use weapons to stop an assault upon property. Three of the admitted police killings were the very first night. While attention has been focused on the corner where the police withdrew and the truck driver was terribly beaten (but rescued by other Blacks), 30 Metro Division cops, including SWAT teams, descended on a single housing project that very night, killing two.

The media management of the news began to get results on the very first day. According to a San Francisco Bay area radio station, national TV talk programs were getting a 3-to-1

Why L.A. Happened

viewer response against the acquittal verdict the morning of the day after it was handed down. But, by evening, the opinions coming in were no more than evenly divided. A solid day of focusing on looting, in pictures and commentary, and on the brutal beating of the white truck-driver, had done its job.

The concealment of the police role by some publications was simply filthy (that it was racist goes without saying). On May 11, the *Los Angeles Times* ran a special 12-page section, equivalent in wordage to an entire book, on the background of the "riots." It went through the entire history of the city, with excellent treatment of the record of police brutality in the past, up until the very eve of the verdict. It interviewed 21 citizens, more African Americans and Latinos than white, of all social strata, women and men, on their experiences during the days after the verdict came down. It reported, accurately and colorfully, statements by African Americans justifying their participation in the spontaneous rebellion in all its forms. But, it did not contain one word on shootings by police subsequent to the verdict, despite the police admission of numerous killings by officers!

In a separate story on three funerals of victims, the *L.A. Times* (May 7) carefully chose to report on individuals not killed by police or whose assailants were unknown. Only two weeks later, on May 24, 26 days after the first killings, did it carry a case-by-case story on the victims of law enforcement officers. But it still did not challenge or so much as look into the claim that the 30 other civilian deaths by gunfire were not at the hands of law enforcement. And on July 12, the *San Francisco Examiner-Chronicle* reported that there had been "no confirmed drive-by shootings between black gangs since the riots" nor, in fact, for six weeks before, thanks to the truce between the Crips and the Bloods. So there is now no alternative explanation to the conclusion that the police killed those 30 people.

A new radical American Left can perform no more noble

service, can do nothing more effective to build a bridge to the most downtrodden and suppressed than to bend its efforts to establishing the true picture of Los Angeles 1992 as police brutality at the level of massacre. This must make clear to the public that its initial reaction to the verdict was correct. America's police forces must some day truly be made the protectors of the people. As a first step, they must be brought under control, with criminals in blue fired and prosecuted. (One cop, Michael Daly, who killed a Salvadoran the second night of the rebellion, had fatally shot an African American in 1987, rousing protests that caused even Chief Gates (!) to criticize him. Daly was ordered then to undergo remedial training, including instruction in the escalation of force.) The rest must be re-educated against racism, and all levels—the rank and file, the middle command and the top—must be brought fully into accord with the demographics of each community.

Broadcast May 19, 1992 on KPFA, Pacifica, Berkeley. Data in this text subsequently updated to July 12.

WILLIAM MANDEL, Jewish, was in the bodyguard at Paul Robeson's Peekskill "Riot" concert, ran for Congress on a ticket headed by Dr. DuBois for Senate, went South in a "premature" Freedom Ride to defend the Martinsville Seven against racist justice in 1951 and traveled the nation promoting William L. Patterson's *We Charge Genocide* (against African Americans) petition to the United Nations. In the 1960s, Mandel was on the editorial board of *The Movement*, the official publication of the Student Non-Violent Coordinating Committee. *(The appelation, "Jewish," was included at the author's request. Ed.)*

The ABC's of Violence:

The Impact of the Rodney King Affair on Black Children

Donna Williams

The great words worker and theoretician on the shenanigans of the global white contenders, Neeley Fuller, Jr., once wondered aloud at the beginning of a seminar why he had to be there, teaching us about white supremacy. Why couldn't he be, he asked impatiently, out on a boat, floating and enjoying the day? Why, in these latter days of the 20th century, did he *still* have to teach about this most distasteful subject? Why hadn't we gotten the lesson?

When the four white police officers who were videotaped bludgeoning Rodney King were unabashedly pronounced not guilty on all charges, I asked myself the same questions. Here was yet another fine mess I had to explain to my six year-old son, Michael. Why, in 1992, did police brutality and white injustice *still* have to be a part of his education? *What* was I going to say? *How* would I tell him? More importantly, how would he react?

Why L.A. Happened

These are some of the questions all conscious, concerned Black parents, teachers, ministers, social workers and community activists must ask themselves. How will the repeatedly televised image of an unarmed Black man being kicked and hit and spat upon and cursed—not to mention the acquittal of his torturers—register in the highly impressionable minds of our Black children? How will this episode make them *feel*?

Black children are being hypnotized into believing that violence is not only a normal, acceptable way of life, but that they deserve to be kicked, hit, spat upon and cursed. The verdicts handed down in the cases of the four white LAPD's, Latasha Harlin and others sanction violence against Black people. Do not underestimate the mind of a Black child: it will absorb this information, much of it unconsciously, process it and, if allowed to stew unchallenged, come to conclusions that will leave them pessimistic about the future.

According to Jeral Constance Muhammad, founder, Life Mastery Dynamics behavior modification seminars,

> In comparisons of African babies to European babies, Black babies have been shown to reflect highly developed motor skills and intellectual ability until around two years of age. And we know that by then, because of how the mind responds to the establishment of the screening mechanism, the reticular activating system, that whatever they have been dominantly exposed to up until around age two has gone in unscreened until that mechanism is established. By that time, habits have become formed. What's happening is our babies are being bombarded with negative racial propaganda, poor diet and poverty, so that between the ages of one-one half and two, mental and motor functioning begins to reverse in favor of the white child.

TV VIOLENCE AND A BOWL OF POPCORN

When TV is the babysitter ("Black households watch an

average of 74 hours of television a week, compared with 51 hours for other households...." *American Demographics*, 1/89), Black children are being cared for and nourished by a lethal visual feast of pimps, prostitutes, junkies, uncommitted buppies, misogynist rappers, Tarzan reruns, weak fathers, white-children-loving "mammies" juxtaposed against "blonde bombshells," disrespectful children, attractively packaged sugar-laden candies and war toys, among other things.

While violence is an unfortunate reality in the lives of many of our children, contrary to media-generated popular opinion, there are many others who have never witnessed or committed a violent act, nor do they know anyone who has. These two sets and further subsets of Black children will undoubtedly process televised fictional violence differently. Studies abound on the effects of violence on children, but three clear possibilities emerge: (1) children will either become so desensitized to violence that they will become passive and apathetic; (2) they will respond by fantasizing or acting out aggressive acts; or, (3) as George Gerbner, Annenberg School of Communications, University of Pennsylvania, and others have discovered, they will manifest feelings of "pervasive insecurity," vulnerability and the need for protection. ("Is TV Violence Battering Our Kids?", *TV Guide*, 8/22-28/92) I'm inclined to believe that all psychoses can manifest in a child simultaneously; regardless, the implications are frightening.

So, if my son watches *Teenage Mutant Ninja Turtles* or old reruns of *Miami Vice*, if the next day at school a friend describes how someone on his block got shot, if he sees a young Black man spread eagle against a police car, then if he overhears his father relating how he had been arrested because he 'fit the description,' it is evident that the various elements of society (including the media) are conspiring to hypnotize my son (yes, it's a conspiracy) into believing that violence is a normal, acceptable way of life.

But I'm fighting it. A couple of years ago, Michael and I

were going home one evening from work and school, driving down the Dan Ryan expressway in Chicago, when suddenly he pointed to the sky and said, "Look, Mama, a gun!"

I looked up and sure enough, to my horror, was a gun. A white man (god-like, high in the sky) in a blue suit, TV name "Hunter," was aiming the gun at all the Black people on the south side of Chicago. He threatened us from a billboard, and the tagline encouraged people to watch his show on Super Channel 9, presumably to see him point his gun at others.

Blue was an interesting choice of color. *Blue* is the color of Chicago's police, the same "to serve and protect" force that is known internationally to *hunt* down Black men and throw them against cars, walls—whatever's handy—then lock 'em up. And, as the recent reports about police commander John Burge allege, some Black men are even being tortured.

To qualify for this treatment, all a body has to do is fit the description—be Black and male. In the eyes of the hunters, they all look alike—the tall, dark ones match the short, light ones. Ask any Black man in Chicago, New York, Rodney King's city—anywhere in the U.S.—if this is indeed a fact of life. A friend of the tall, dark variety claims he's been harassed so many times that he's on a first-name basis with the entire Chicago force. All jokes aside, policemen are threats to Black men as a group, and consequently Black women and children, and what am I supposed to teach my son when he sees one pointing a gun at him from a picture high in the sky? Or when he sees several cops beating a Black man senseless on TV—and it's not pretend this time?

Well, it seems he figured it out, because immediately after seeing the gun on the billboard, my son said, "Ma, guns are bad. Don't you wish he didn't have one?"

Yes, I wish that Hunter didn't have one. Armed white men—even mere pictures of them—bother me. I don't know, just call it a vague, hazy feeling that somebody Black is about to get killed. Am I paranoid?

The ABC's of Violence: The Impact of the Rodney King Affair on Black Children

After we meditated on the evil of guns, particularly in the hands of white policemen, Michael said, shaking his head sadly: "Guns, beer and cigarette ads. Why do they put them up there, Ma?"

In one brilliant flash of mind, my son had synthesized the negative impact of all the seemingly unrelated images as killers. All of them. He did not see them as separate media events, but as one combined threat. I was so proud of him. Our African ancestors used this wholistic style of thinking to build the pyramids.

All parents need to fight against the hypnosis that the media is trying to perpetrate on their children. And while violence and substance abuse may be the way of American life—and our children need to know about them in no uncertain terms—I absolutely refuse to let him think that this madness is normal.

RODNEY KING, ROLE MODEL?

Because of the videotape and the international coverage it received, the name "Rodney King" is now synonymous with police brutality. The world convulsed in horror as it watched this Black man's beating. (Even Jeffrey Dahmer was treated more gently by police.) So-called "Rodney King Riots" erupted in cities throughout the world when the decision of the Simi Valley jury was released.

For Black people, Rodney King is more than a symbol, he is one of us. Our hearts went out to him when we saw him in that wheelchair, face bloated, dried blood everywhere. When he said $1 million for every blow that he took, we said, "Gone, brother."

We adults understand Rodney King. We can keep him in perspective. As for children, well, that's something else.

If ever there was an anti-hero, Rodney King's it. He's the quintessential ne'er-do-well who just can't seem to get it together. His past involvements with the police are legendary, and although irrelevant to the beating, his behavior on the road leading up to it is questionnable. Subsequent to the beating and verdict, King has continued to have run-ins with the LAPD.

The point is, when it comes to children, we've got to be careful about those whom we set before them as role models. The phenomenon of Rodney King is complex, and our children must be given the whole story.

STAR SPANGLED BOMBERS

Violence is nothing new to America. It is written into the very fabric of the red, white and blue:

> *...and the rockets red glare*
> *the bombs bursting in air*
> *gave proof through the night*
> *that our flag was still there...*

Nor is violence—real or fantasy—on TV new. Indeed, mere babes may be more sophisticated in their viewing than their parents. Aletha Huston, co-director of the Center for Research on the Influence of Television on Children, says that "...children may see more violence on commercial television than their parents do; adult programs have an average of 5 violent acts per hour, while children's programming averages 15 to 25...." (*Christianity Today*, 2/17/89) In a study conducted by the Center for Media and Public Affairs and commissioned by *TV Guide*, cartoons were discovered to be the most violent program form, with an astounding 471 scenes tabulated across an 18-hour period. (*TV Guide*, 8/22-28/92)

Even the coverage of *real* violence—violence that has occurred to or by some living human being—is not new. Every night, the news features plenty of gore for even the toughest of stomachs. This type of violence, like the *Miami Vice-Ninja Turtle* variety, is a high tech production: a commentator narrates the action; editing technology allows writers and directors to skim the surface of a story, weeding out (or including) various salient elements. Contrary to the journalistic credo, there is no such thing as objective reporting, especially when the newsrooms are run by a couple dozen corporations owned by the white global contenders. (Ben H. Bagdikian, *The Media Monopoly*, 1990)

From drive-by shootings, domestic strife and gang killings to war, the news [MUSIC UP] *brings it all to you*. Desert Storm, for example, was the war that innovated the new Nintendo-style reporting. Many networks created music and graphics to enhance the Middle East war theater. We saw the bombs dropping, but we didn't see the people, which further drove a wedge between feelings and acts of violence—State supported violence at that, with the American flag held on high as the ultimate symbol of the aggression.

But the genius of children lies in their ability to call the emperor out when he's walking around butt naked. When my son saw the constant images of the flag linked together with the machines of war, Michael saw no abstract ideas like "freedom" or "liberation" cloaking the flag. He did see tanks and war planes and bombs and made the only logical conclusion: the American flag is a war flag.

So violence, real or fictionalized, on TV is not new. What is a relatively new phenomenon, however, is the airing of a videotaped act of real violence—*uncut and unedited*. The tape of Rodney King's beating was powerful because the pain of the man lying on the ground and the barbarism of the police officers literally jumped off the screen in this raw footage. There was no artistry in the making of this tape. No gel lighting, no multitude of angles, no quick cuts, no hair-starched anchor commentating, no catchy tunes. Just one lone camera steady on the action. Quiet as it's kept, in the archives of any self-respecting television station are hundreds and hundreds of tapes of raw footage with that same ability to squeeze emotion out of the stoniest of hearts. Instead of letting them stand on their own, unanalyzed and unedited, they are spliced and diced into neatly packaged pieces for whatever the Corporation wants you, the viewer, to believe. Raw footage is Truth; technically manipulated coverage of events may or may not be.

That raw Rodney King tape shocked Black folks out of their media-induced apathy. People who lean towards aggression and hostility when watching shows like *Predator* or *Hunter* wanted to kill when the verdict was announced. This group wanted to blow something up; they sympathized and cheered the brothers and sisters who took to the streets.

Son Michael, who tends to psychologically process the day-to-day TV violence to internalize both apathy and aggression (which is why I've had to severely cut his viewing time), now talks about killing white people. Now, I am nonviolent by nature, but like Malcolm said, how are you going to be nonviolent with a people who insist on being violent with you?

Michael is basically peaceful and fun-loving by nature, but on this one subject, for him, there is no compromise—you kill people who are killing you. He sees white people as the bad guys, and I am hard pressed to tell him otherwise.

LET THE HEALING BEGIN

One sunny Friday in May back in 1988, a crazy white woman named Laurie Dann waltzed into Hubbard Woods Grade School in Winnetka, Illinois and started shooting children. As *People Weekly* (6/6/88) reported, "Within 30 minutes of the shootings...psychologists, social workers and clergy were racing to the scene. So began Winnetka's remarkable communal effort to heal the mental wounds...."

When Black children saw Rodney King getting the stew beat out of him over and over again, and when later they heard that the criminals had been acquitted, the damage was as devastating as if a Laurie Dann had put a bullet in their heads.

Where are the psychologists, social workers and clergy (of all denominational stripes) to help our children sort out this

The ABC's of Violence: The Impact of the
Rodney King Affair on Black Children

mess? Where are the programs? *Within 30 damn minutes* help was on the way for those Winnetka children. By the time this book is on the stands, it will have been months since the verdict, over a year since the actual beating, and I can only hope that some programs have been put into place to help Black children cope with this ugly American episode and the continuing problems we face with white-on-Black violence. Will we leave the healing of our children to the likes of Nickelodeon?

In the meantime, I've got to do it. Once again I'm forced to talk to my son about white violence and injustice when I'd rather be out on a boat soaking up the sun. I recalled our discussions of Nelson Mandela's release. I had told him all about the barbaric white South Africans who had locked up Mandela nearly three decades ago, how they mistreated him—just like the white LAPD did to Rodney King. Again, I had no other choice but to tell him the truth of what happened to King. In my home, no matter how painful the truth is, it will not be a casualty of war. Besides, if children are sheltered from the harsh realities of life in America, they will be unprepared for the evils (drugs, harmful media images, police brutality, gang drafts, etc.) that inevitably will come searching for them.

Days later after we talked, Michael raised that issue of killing white people, but initially, he didn't have much to say. While I was explaining what had happened to King, his eyes grew wide, but that was about all. Already, at six years old some emotional dulling has set in, and I don't know what to do about it. Considering the ache that living in this violent society wreaks upon body, mind and spirit, maybe it's for the best.

DONNA WILLIAMS is Senior Editor at Third World Press and Managing Editor, *Black Books Bulletin*. She is completing a book about deprogramming children from the harmful effects of media.

part four . . .

ATLANTA: WHAT HAPPENED TO THE NEW SOUTH?

Postscript to the Los Angeles Riot:

Atlanta and the Crisis of

Black Leadership

Tiffany Patterson

The acquittal of the four white police officers who were accused of beating Rodney King in Los Angeles ignited the rage and frustration that has been seething in America's inner cities for more than two decades. The media coverage and commentary attempted to paint the riot that followed the verdict as a *Black reaction,* but the images and newspaper coverage make it clear that the rioting included white and Latino participants. What is clear, too, is that most Americans were outraged and shocked by the verdict. This consensus cut across class and racial lines.

Leaders both Black and white called for calm, arguing that violence was not the way to address social concerns. President Bush, whose lack of domestic policy and extreme insensitivity to the nation's poor has been a hallmark of both his and Ronald Reagan's administrations, mounted a moral hobby horse, condemning the violence and attempting to deny its source. In a televised speech on Friday, May 1, Bush stated:

What we saw last night and the night before in Los

Angeles is not about civil rights. It's not about the great cause of equality that all Americans must uphold. It's not a message of protest. It's been the brutality of a mob, pure and simple.

Of course, political leaders, particularly those who create the conditions for mob violence, cannot acknowledge that riots are never pure and simple. The riot in Los Angeles, like other riots that have peppered the American historical landscape for two hundred years, expose the seething undercurrent of hostility, disharmony and discontent that rests just beneath the surface of calm and progress that outlines America's image. It is the last resort of the frustrated and the disenfranchised.

The verdict, too, exposed not only the frustration in Los Angeles, but the depth of poverty and racial tension across the country. Demonstrations took place in several cities across the country, including New York, NY, Washington, DC, Chicago, IL, Minneapolis, MN, Denver, CO, Kansas City, MO, Topeka, KS, Amherst, MS and Hartford, CT. The windshields of 34 police cars were shattered in Madison, Wisconsin with a note at the scene that read "Justice for King." Most of the cities in the South remained fairly calm, except for Atlanta. Atlanta literally exploded with rage.

When news of the verdict and the subsequent demonstrations in Los Angeles reached across the country, students at the Atlanta University Center (Clark-Atlanta University, Morris-Brown College, Morehouse College, Spelman College and the Interdenominational Theological Seminary) organized a demonstration to express their outrage and anger, a peaceful demonstration which turned violent, leaving more than $800,000 in damaged property in downtown Atlanta. Several people were beaten, including a 45 year-old white man attempting to get home from work. The following day, student leaders attempted to organize a peaceful demonstration on campus.

Atlanta police and the Georgia Bureau of Investigation

Why L.A. Happened

—on orders from Mayor Maynard Jackson—invaded the campuses of AUC and turned a peaceful demonstration into a confrontation. Students were pushed and shoved, and tear gas was shot into dormitories. According to student spokespersons, the students began throwing rocks and tin cans after police shoved a young woman, knocking her to the ground. The riot spilled out from the campus, and community businesses were looted in the melee that followed. The visual image reminded one of Soweto, South Africa. The miracle was that no one was killed, although many were injured.

In a series of meetings held on campus and in the wake of criticism of the city government from several of the college presidents, faculty and administrators, students demanded accountability from the Mayor. The Mayor's response was to attempt to control the student response by plying them with cliches about non-violence while he made clear his intent to protect white business interests at the expense of human lives and the right to protest and assembly. Invoking the name of Dr. King, Jackson and his supporters suggested that the students were ignorant of King's message of non-violence and chided them for not sticking to their books.

In what has become a shameful distortion of history, the political elite have appropriated Dr. King's leadership and *dream* as a means of silencing criticism and repressing overt protest. Even before the Atlanta riot, in the context of the King Birthday celebrations that are held every year, Dr. King's image had been carefully crafted as a *dream* and limited to his "I Have A Dream" speech of 1963, ignoring his biting criticism of the American system and his growing political radicalism in the five years between 1963 and 1968. In this manner, Dr. King's life has been made available as both a tool for repression and progress.

In Atlanta, a significant sector of the Africanamerican political elite has proceeded to become nothing more than the sycophants for the white business community. Indeed, this is understandable, for the stakes are very high. The 1996 Olympics means more to the Atlanta elite than the wrenching poverty that plagues most Black residents. In distorting King's message, Jackson's administration ignored King's commitment to civil disobedience, albeit non-violent. More importantly, King never advocated state-sanctioned violence. In unleashing the police on students at AUC, Jackson precipitated a riot and suppressed the right to protest.

The contradictions of history were not lost on many students. When Jackson came to campus and attempted to explain his position and present them with a three point *program*, his comments fell on deaf ears. Many students walked out the gym, leaving other officials, such as County Commissioner Michael Lomax, alone on the stage. Doug Elliard, a 21 year-old Morehouse junior majoring in political science, captured the understanding that began dawning on many students. His comments in the *Atlanta Journal/Constitution* bear repeating at length:

> Atlanta has developed into a beautiful city—for white people. I can't say the same for African Americans. I don't see the same progress being achieved in our community as I do in others. I see my people being displaced out of their homes for Olympic Games that are four years away...
>
> The strategy of non-violence is worn out. It has not brought significant benefits to African Americans since its heyday in the 1960s. Even at that time, it was not the only strategy of the civil rights movement. People have forgotten that Dr. King's methods would not have been as effective were it not for the threat of violence articulated by leaders such as Malcolm X. Malcolm's insistence that African Americans respect themselves and stand up against injustice seems especially relevant today...

Why L.A. Happened

It is not a question of choosing between violence and non-violence. It is a matter of realizing that if we hope to achieve real progress, we cannot have too much of one strategy without the other...

The Bush Administration says it will look into the filing of federal charges against the four Los Angeles police officers. This is typical of the superficial actions that are taken just to pacify us. There are no plans for genuine change. Two years from now, everything will be exactly the same...

If Atlanta is committed to social change, then why did its leaders show more concern about how last week's events would affect the city's image than about the needs of African Americans?

Elliard, like many students, are beginning to critique the class divisions with the Black community. Though many still limit their analysis to race, others are beginning to unpack the complex relationship between race and class. Increasingly, students and political analysts are being forced to confront the contradictions of class within the Africanamerican community.

The image of Atlanta as a city of *brotherly love*, as *The City Too Busy to Hate*, was shattered after the Los Angeles riots and the rift among Black leadership rose to the surface. Jackson attempted to give the appearance of unity by calling a meeting of civic leaders from the business and political community. But not all were willing to pretend that this riot was merely an aberration of misguided students. Rep. Mabel Thomas (D-Atlanta) lamented, "LA burns and the fire inside all of us simmers. Simmers from despair, simmers from anger and simmers from hopelessness." Elizabeth Omilami, the daughter of civil rights activist Hosea Williams stated, "The frustrations are much higher in Atlanta than many of us want to admit because we have the appearance of prosperity in the black community. Atlanta's image as the African American mecca is not what the reality is for most blacks here."

Atlanta indeed has a burgeoning Black middle class and a wealth of Black elected officials. But economically, Atlanta ranks in the category of Newark, New Jersey, as being one of the poorest cities in America. There are two Black cities in Atlanta: one wealthy, one poor. Reginald Eaves, former Fulton County Commissioner, acknowledges that the gap between these communities fueled the upheaval. "There are two distinct societies; two totally different black communities in Atlanta. Atlanta's elite bourgeois have totally alienated the downtrodden, they can't identify with many of us." And local talk show host Dave Walker, who is also a vendor in downtown Atlanta, observed "there is a bitter class struggle being waged in the black community that is far worse than anything we witnessed in the 1960s. At one end are fat cat black elected officials and their business buddies who are routinely portrayed as profiting from the system. And, at the other end of the spectrum are most black folks who are totally disconnected from the system."

Mayors in other cities, like Dinkins in New York and Pratt in Washington, DC, acknowledged the legitimate rage and need to publicly protest among the residents in their cities. In doing so, they were able to limit the degree of violence by providing a valve for the anger to escape momentarily. Other leaders, like California Congresswoman Maxine Waters, refused to be drawn into focusing only on the violence but insisted instead on underscoring the oppressive forces which have destroyed people's lives, leaving them little alternative but violence. Not so Maynard Jackson. His approach was to silence all protest in a frantic effort to keep Atlanta's image clean and by extension, his own.

It became clear that business leaders were more concerned with their image, not the social problems of Atlanta's citizens. Thomas stated, "I don't think we've ever really and truly embraced the spirit nor substance of the slogan, 'The City Too Busy to Hate.' The privileged in [suburban] Buckhead

Why L.A. Happened

Too Busy to Hate.' The privileged in [suburban] Buckhead certainly don't feel comfortable with the poor from Buckhead. And, that includes Mayor [Maynard] Jackson, who lives the good life in Buckhead and can't possibly relate to the hopelessness and apprehension that consumes the black community."

The divisions in Atlanta cannot be understood simply in racial terms. A bitter class struggle is being waged in Atlanta, and the Simi Valley verdict exposed the scope of that struggle. In Atlanta, perhaps more than any other major American city, Blacks have abandoned the city for the suburbs. The mark of success and middle-class status is living outside of the city. By the thousands, Africanamericans have moved away from the visual reality of poverty and despair. They drive in for jobs and leave quickly to avoid being tainted by the physical manifestation of decay—the homeless, the jobless, the infirm.

In the wake of this flight, a mentality has been constructed. This mentality has blinded middle-class Africanamericans, to borrow a phrase from Mario Cuomo, to the "quiet catastrophes" that are erupting daily in the city and allows these suburbanites of color to see the inhabitants in the city as *those people*. And the system restricts the options of this group by providing less expensive housing and better police protection in the suburbs than the city. For example, students at the AUC campuses are poorly protected by the city, and often, students are killed in drive-by shootings and robbery attempts. The police in the city with a Black Mayor has not only refused to provide adequate protection but has shifted the blame for the lack of protection onto the Colleges.

Mayor Jackson's and city officials' sending of troops onto the AUC campuses was designed to protect the carefully crafted image of Atlanta as "The City Too Busy to Hate." But the violence exposed the festering underbelly of Atlanta. The image sought to hide the wrenching poverty and constant violence that is the reality for the majority of Black Atlantans.

Instead, the Black political elite have worked hard to paint a picture of racial harmony and progress while scores of Atlantans, both Black and white, struggle daily against joblessness, homelessness and hopelessness. This reality is even more startling in a city which can boast considerable representation in government, business and civic affairs. The riots exposed the contradictions of Black political leadership that has failed to address the fundamental needs of Black people and instead has been content to applaud the success of the middle- and upper-class elite. The particular history of Atlanta provides a laboratory for examining the failure of Africanamerican leadership and mechanisms by which capitalism continues to maintain hegemonic control. Though the media continues to interpret the riots in Los Angeles and Atlanta within the paradigm of race relations, the political structure makes clear that this analysis alone is no longer adequate. A simple race analysis is not sufficient to explain the actions of an Africanamerican mayor and leadership. Class and its contradictions in the Black community must also be examined.

Thinkers, activists and political leaders must begin to address these issues if we are going to salvage the human potential of our communities, create a new political leadership and address the roots of the blight that affect our communities. The diversity of opinion and ideological positions that these incidents have exposed is not necessarily a negative development.

For too long, Africanamericans have attempted to maintain a smooth public face of unity, denying the ever present ideological and class differences within the community. And that public face has more often than not been a more moderate one in spite of the presence of more radical voices. In view of the virulent racism that shaped the political struggle of Africanamericans, such a public face was necessary, so many believed. But this need for unity has prevented the internal criticism needed to hold leaders accountable. As a consequence, we do not have the foundation for the kind of public political discourse needed to allow us to make complicated and informed decisions and to prevent our community from being the pawns of capitalists and racist political interests. The race card is being played by forces hostile to the interests of Africanamericans.

In other words, a simple race analysis too often overrides all other considerations. This was evident in a dramatic way in the public response to the nomination of Clarence Thomas to the Supreme Court. Many Africanamericans could not see beyond his gender or race to acknowledge that his ideological position was consistent with white male patriarchy and not the interests of the majority of Africanamericans, other ethnic minorities, all poor people and women.

Leaders at all levels of society—politicians, activists, teachers, intellectuals, entrepreneurs, etc.—must be held accountable and operate in the best interest of the people they serve and from whom they draw their legitimacy. When they fail to operate in this manner, they must be exposed for their opportunism and the basis of their legitimacy withdrawn. What is in the best interest of the community can only be determined by involving a wide range of people crossing class, gender and age lines in both a public and private discourse. This determination cannot be left to the elite few, and leaders like Maynard Jackson should not be allowed to lecture to students, yet fail to engage them in public debate.

Consensus must be struggled for; it is not automatically given. That struggle must include and respect the opinions of male and female workers, students, youth, professionals, the homeless, jobless, aged, welfare mothers, etc.—in short, all sectors of the society. The critical discourse that will come from such a struggle will make clear whose interests are being served, and on this basis political positions can be fought for and won. Too often, those in leadership positions believe that they can learn nothing from those whom they serve. The art of listening is born in humility, and it is time for leaders to listen to those who bear the brunt of violence and economic oppression.

Hope has been born from the violence in Los Angeles and Atlanta. Students were jolted out of their complacency, and new leaders made their appearance. New organizations concerned with social justice were formed on campus, and the public was shocked into attention. To keep this flicker of hope alive, however, leaders must seize the moment to evaluate the direction of leadership and with humility, seek answers from the people they serve. The populace must also seize the moment and evaluate their leaders more critically and with courage withdraw legitimacy from those who fail them and be accountable for their own complacency. If we do not take this opportunity for a revitalized struggle, the future of our children will be forfeited. The historical moment demands our attention and demands that we listen.

TIFFANY PATTERSON teaches history at Spelman College in Atlanta.

A Luta Continua:

"It Was Either This Or Nothing."

Kalamu ya Salaam interviews Kiini Ibura Salaam, one of the leaders of the Atlanta student response to the "Rodney King" verdict.

"Each generation must out of relative obscurity discover its mission, fulfill it, or betray it."
— Frantz Fanon, *The Wretched Of The Earth*

Most media commentary on the Los Angeles rebellion and the aftermath has come from "observers" rather than the participants themselves. In fact, for many of us who are over forty, there was no real outrage, just a cynical knowing that business was going on as usual in America. But for the youth, this was a watershed event, a coming of age that signifies the end of the philosophical acceptance of integration and the belief that the system can be modified to accept and serve our interests.

This is the moment of generational reckoning about which Fanon so eloquently spoke. Following the announcement of the verdict, there were demonstrations, rallies or marches at nearly every Black college in the country. In most cases they were "peaceful," however, at the six-college Atlanta University Complex (Atlanta University, Clark, Morehouse, Morris Brown, Spelman and Union Theological Seminary), the

185

Why L.A. Happened

citadel of "Negro higher education," there were two days of major disturbances. The importance of these demonstrations was largely ignored by the media.

At 4:30am following the verdict, my daughter, Kiini Ibura Salaam, a 19 year-old sophomore at Spelman, called to tell me the students had demonstrated all night and planned to march downtown later that day. I encouraged her, wished her safety and waited to hear more. It was Saturday before I spoke to her again, and by then Atlanta was prime time news. When Kiini returned home at the end of the semester, we talked about what happened in Atlanta and why. Here is a report from the field, from one of the people who helped to organize the Atlanta response to the not guilty verdict.

KALAMU: Atlanta was one of the places where there were major demonstrations and so-called "outbreaks of violence." That took many people by surprise. In Los Angeles the demonstrations were primarily street oriented, and most of the participants were neighborhood people, meaning residents of the inner city. In Atlanta most of the demonstrations, or at least the way the demonstrations were projected in the media, were comprised of so-called middle-class college students from some of the more prestigious Black universities in the country. You were involved in those demonstrations. Let's talk about the demonstrations in Atlanta from your perspective. Why do you think Atlanta erupted the way it did?

KIINI: I guess the real reason was the college students—not that the people who live there wouldn't have done anything, but most of the violence that happened was a result of college students actively protesting.

The night of the verdict I was at a party. We were watching it on tv. I don't really know how we took it initially. We watched it. We talked about it. We were angry. And then we danced. So we couldn't have been all that affected. I don't know whether we were thinking about it, processing it, or whether we just didn't feel like dealing with it at that point, but we were dancing. Then we heard a lot of people go by. They had marched from the AUC (Atlanta University Center). It was a spur of the moment kind of thing.

I am sure one or two people started the march, but it was very spontaneous. Like, "come on, let's go downtown."

KALAMU: Why downtown?

KIINI: I have no idea. I know the person who claims to have started the march, and I didn't really talk to him about it because we were dealing with so many other things. Perhaps downtown because the police headquarters was there, and that's where people were.

Everybody left the party and joined the march. The police were ready. I guess they had seen what happened in Los Angeles. We went down to the capitol building. It was around 1:00 in the morning. The police had two cars behind us and were stationed at all the corners. When we turned the corner to approach one of the capitol buildings the street was filled with police. In general the police were very calm with us. They were just watching us.

On the way to the capitol building, some people were knocking down garbage cans, they were throwing things, they tried to break some windows—

KALAMU: Who were "they"? The student demonstrators?

KIINI: Some of the male students.

KALAMU: Why do you say "male" students?

KIINI: Because that's the people who were throwing things and knocking down things. We got to Georgia State, and

187

one guy started screaming "fuck Georgia State" and wanted to break their windows. In general, it wasn't the group. It was maybe five or so out of over a hundred who were doing that. Some of us were trying to control the people who wanted to throw things. It was pretty organized to the extent that something spontaneous can be. The leaders were trying to keep people together, not to have anybody straggling behind, and they seemed obsessed with this thing about trying to keep the sisters in the middle, like they were prepared to protect us.

As soon as we got to the capitol, someone rushed to the building and tried to break a window. When the cops saw that, the cops rushed toward the crowd. Half the crowd ran away and half remained. This is the point where organization becomes important. What do you do when the cops rush you? Me and my friends were trying to tell people "just sit down." And so we stayed on the stairs, and at that point it had not been decided what we were going to do.

By the time 3:00 came the police had detained two people. They detained one person because he tried to break the window. I don't know why they detained the other person. There was a small group trying to decide what to do. My friends and I were sitting down. There was a news reporter with a camera trying to find a woman to speak. Nobody wanted to speak, so I said, I'll speak. One of the guys said, "don't let her exploit you. Don't get on tv." For some reason the men didn't want me, a woman, to speak. They felt like they had the right to stop me from speaking. While I was speaking one of the guys actually put his hands over the camera to try to stop me from speaking. I don't know why. Men had said what they needed to say. After they heard what I had to say, people started saying, let her speak, let her speak.

KALAMU: What did you say?

KIINI: The reporter wanted to know why we were out there. I said to protest the blatant racism. Of course, we knew this has been going on, but the fact that there was tangible evidence that the whole nation saw and those officers were still acquited was like throwing our powerlessness in our face. My girlfriend also spoke to the reporters.

After that, the leader who had started the march wanted to go to the precinct to get the two brothers out. I said, how are you going to do that? He didn't know. He said, well we'll just ask. I said, if not, what then? He said, we'll do whatever we have to. I said, what is that? They didn't know. These little crises illustrated a problem within our generation. We don't know tactics and organizational techniques for effective demonstrations, such as, what to do when the police rush, what to do when the march gets to the destination, how to get demonstrators out of jail. Anyway, half the group starts walking toward the precinct and half stays. When they saw that we were staying, they came back to try to convince us.

KALAMU: At that point, did any of the people return who had run when the police charged?

KIINI: No. But we had a nice number of people still there. I wish I knew how to estimate numbers better. It looked like to me it was about fifty people who ran, but we still had a significant number. We covered the entire stairs of the building. They still had cops all over. There was one middle-aged man telling us to go home and pray, and he was also communicating with the police. There were still some hotheads, but in general people were just talking about what we should do.

KALAMU: Describe what happened when the police charged. What did they do?

KIINI: They pulled out their billy clubs and ran toward the most concentrated area of people. They hit one or two of the brothers, but they didn't do anything to us. When they charged, whoever ran is whom they followed behind.

The first time they rushed us, they came from both the street on the side of us and from the top of the stairs above us. The second rush came from other police who had remained at the top of the stairs. They started down the stairs toward us. We sat down. But some people started scattering and panicking. To me, that's how we lost a lot of the people.

KALAMU: Why did you decide to sit down?

KIINI: Number one, I wasn't trying to get hurt, and it seemed like the most logical thing I could do to protect myself. They couldn't beat me up if I was just sitting down. Well, they could, but they wouldn't have any justification. Number two, it didn't make any sense to just run. I had done nothing. I guess from you and mama I just knew that I didn't have to run, and it didn't make any sense to run. Also, I really didn't believe they were going to do anything to us. Had they wanted to, they would have done it before. They let us have that march. They let us stand on those stairs. I know that. I wasn't afraid that they were going to intentionally hurt us.

Finally, our "leader" decided that we needed to go back to campus, regroup and come back.

KALAMU: Who was the leader?

KIINI: He was a Morehouse student named Joel. I don't know his last name. Don't ask me why he was the leader. He was hyper. He was speaking forcefully, and he appealed to the people.

At one point after we got there, he said we needed to go get the brothers out. Then, fifteen minutes later, he said, I don't know about yall, but I'm going to sit here and stay all night til dawn and then try to disrupt the business in the morning. Then, ten minutes later, he's saying we need to go back to the campus and regroup. That was three different plans in less than one hour, so if we're following him, we're in trouble. I felt like, we were there. We had a significant number of people. It was 4:00 in the morning, we didn't have that much time to wait, we could have just stayed there. The police didn't force us to leave.

KALAMU: Why did you leave?

KIINI: I left because most of the people followed Joel, and it didn't make much sense for ten people to sit on the stairs. Even if I didn't agree with the plan, the unity was better than having a split with a few of us straggling behind. I told them on the way back that I didn't agree with the decision, but I felt like I needed to stay with the group for both safety and unity.

I don't like to fight to make my ideas heard, even if I think or believe that I'm right or if I have something pertinent to say. People had their emotions running, it was intense, and this is what they'd been romantically dreaming about for so long. I didn't want to fight to get on the megaphone to say what I had to say. Now, however, I feel like I should have, and I feel like I had something important to say.

When we were leaving, there were two white women in a jeep who drove by, and one male threw a bottle at the jeep. I started fussing at them, and they basically ignored me. I was trying to tell them that if we were supposed to be protesting a Black man getting beaten down just because he was Black, you can't throw a bottle at a white person simply because they're white. I know that it was a reaction to everything, but if college students are supposed to be thinkers then we'll have to be bigger than that and not mimic the violence that has been brought against us by white people in general.

If we are protesting injustices, for us to do the same thing weakens the validity of our protest. I think that if we do some kind of violence then it should be directed, it should be at a

191

certain target or for a specific reason or end. But to be walking down a street and throw a bottle at some people in a car, why do that, to what end, what do we gain?

KALAMU: Why do you think it was males throwing the bottles and such?

KIINI: Males are socialized to deal with their anger in a certain way, and women are socialized to deal with anger in a different way. To be a Black man is to be angry. Right now Malcolm X is idolized, but I don't think people really listen to him, even when they sit down and listen to his speeches. I think they already have an idea of what he's saying. I was listening to one of his speeches yesterday, and he kept stressing the fact that "by any means necessary" doesn't mean just go beat somebody up. He means that when they come bomb your house, you have the right to retaliate. He means don't turn the other cheek. He means self defense. He does not mean go out and punch somebody in the face. I believe that people read him, I believe they listen to him, but I don't believe they hear him because they've already decided what "by any means necessary" means.

I think that it was mostly males because they've been taught to deal with their anger in a physical way and on top of that, to be a Black man—to be strong and not "afraid of the white man"—you break things up. It doesn't make any sense, but that's the way men are taught to deal with their anger.

KALAMU: What was the make up of the march Wednesday night, male to female?

KIINI: It was mostly male but not overwhelmingly so. Maybe two-thirds male to one-third female. But we also found out from two women who came up after we had gotten to the capitol that the police were closing the AU area down and not letting people come down.

KALAMU: What happened when you got back to campus?

"It Was Either This Or Nothing."

KIINI: Joel had a meeting in his room. I and my friend Mary Lou went. There were three other females: Bianca, Christin, Shawna. Four guys whom I didn't know and two guys I knew: Agai and Shawn. We tried to plan and determine what would make the most sense. Some people thought we needed to really plan it so that there would be a lot of support and organization. They wanted to have a demonstration on Friday to give us time to organize. But we felt like the interest would not be there if we waited. The Atlanta University Complex is very complacent, and we were all surprised that the students came up and marched.

We decided to have two people go to each campus, call people and tell them what was going on and to meet at the library at a certain time. We wanted to have a rally explaining what we wanted to do. We had planned to go to City Hall and make a statement from the AU center, a challenge to the Mayor and the Governor to publicly denounce the verdict and push for a trial on the federal level. That's what we wanted.

Agai said, "sometimes you have to rip things up." He was, well, not pushing for viole... I don't even like to use the word "violence" because it has been used in the wrong way by the media. What was going on was negative, but it wasn't simply that. It wasn't simply, "I'm going to punch you in the face." There was a lot motivating it. People are fed up, and so sometimes when the media says "violence" they don't incorporate or recognize all the other conditions. They take the act out of context. Anyway, Agai was trying to say that sometimes that's what has to happen because no changes come from non-violent means. I guess most of us were countering that with "there's a time for everything," and at this point that is not something we need or want to do.

The rally was set for 1:00. We went from dorm to dorm.

193

Why L.A. Happened

A lot of people were receptive, but I don't think as many people as we talked with actually showed up. It was finals time. But a lot of people did show up. I'm not good at estimating numbers, but it was at least double what we had the night before. And when we started marching, I looked back, and it was really a lot of people.

Shawn and Joel spoke about the issue, and at that point only one person in the crowd was shouting out disagreement. But before they got to the point of telling people what we wanted to do once we got to city hall, Mukassa (Willie Ricks) came up with his fist in the air shouting "Uhuru, Uhuru." That fired the crowd up, and they started chanting in response. Then some people in the crowd began shouting "let him speak, let him speak." He's respected on Morehouse's campus for his knowledge, commitment and dedication.

I don't want to make his speech sound less than it was.

KALAMU: What do you mean?

KIINI: I didn't like what he did or the way he handled it. I don't want to present it in a biased way. I want to be honest about what he was trying to say, however, all I heard was rhetoric.

KALAMU: What do you mean by "rhetoric"?

KIINI: I mean, there are certain established facts that we know. What we don't know is how to deal with our problems. Essentially he said the "by any means necessary, let's go" rhetoric, and then we marched. But where were we going, what were we going to do? Nobody knew because that had never been announced.

Mukassa had the last word before we marched, but there was no clear plan of action. Even if violence is the action that you want to take, it still needs to be directed and focused. Had he said "we're going to go break the windows of the police station" to me, that would have been a statement. Or, "we're going to turn over every police car that we see." That would have been a statement. But just to turn people loose doesn't say anything but "we're angry," and we know that already.

I guess a lot of white people didn't know that, and to a certain extent they saw how bad it was. Or maybe they didn't, maybe they just said, "look at them running wild." I don't know.

Anyway, we were at the library and went from there to Morehouse's campus and then through all the other campuses. Spelman's campus is closed to males through finals time, but we had so many people, they just let us march through. I don't see what else they could have done because we were picking up people as we marched.

There was a helicopter overhead, just like there was a helicopter on Wednesday night. So after we marched through the campuses, then we went through the neighborhood calling out to people to join us and then headed downtown. At that point some demonstrators broke a window of a neighborhood grocery store. It was a small business which seemed to be Black owned. Why that window was broken I don't know. My girlfriend made a good point: after all this destruction, we get to go home and leave these broken windows and destroyed stores behind, but the people in the neighborhood have to stay and suffer the consequences of our anger.

As we were leaving the neighborhood and approaching MLK Boulevard which leads directly downtown, Shawn and Joel said that Dr. Cole (President of Spelman) supported what we were doing and wanted us to come and speak to her about tactics to take to control the crowd. Now, Shawn and Joel were the people who were supposed to make the statement when we got to City Hall, so I didn't see what good it was going to do for us to leave once the march was already in progress, but we left.

Why L.A. Happened

We went to the library where all the presidents of the schools were meeting. To me, they were talking about the problem of the race in general. They read a statement that the presidents of the school were going to release which denounced the verdict.

But, they still were telling us to have rallies on our individual campuses. "We're responsible for you, don't go tear up downtown." It's hard to say that they were trying to stop us from being heard because I'm sure that's not were they were trying to do. I guess what I realized, that it seemed that others didn't, it was this or nothing. We weren't prepared to do anything else.

KALAMU: Why do you say that?

KIINI: Because a lot of people said that they agreed with the protest but that we were doing it wrong. But when you think about it, had we had little rallies on our campuses, nobody would have heard anything about that. Nobody would have known, and it would not have made any kind of difference. People don't think about, ok, what if it hadn't gone down the way it did, what else was plausible? When you look at the news, what did you see? You saw L.A. for five minutes, then you saw Atlanta for three minutes, and then they flashed real quick, "oh, these are the other marches." They were successful marches. They were big marches. They were of mixed races, white and Black people. They were making a statement, but the news did not give them any play.

That's another thing that people don't think about. The news is not objective. It's slanted. It's sad, but even marches don't matter and, to a certain extent, that's where people who agree with violence have a point. The news decides who's going to get play and who's going to see it and when. They're running the news like it's an action movie. You need a certain amount of bombs, violence or dead bodies to get on the news. They

want to talk about violence, murder, rapes and crack. There is
no interest in just a plain, straightforward statement. And to a
certain extent, that's where I have to give credit to the rioting:
people were heard.

KALAMU: So Joel, Shawn and you left the demonstration before it got downtown to go talk with Dr. Cole and the
other presidents. Why were you asked to go? Had you been
designated or elected as one of the three leaders?

KIINI: I really don't know, they asked me to go. I guess
because I was part of the planning, or maybe they considered
me a rational person. I know I was constantly challenging them.
The reason they invited me to the planning meeting in the first
place is because I was complaining so much the first night. I
kept saying, we shouldn't be leaving, why are we leaving? They
said, the leaders decided, and I said, who are the leaders and
who chose them? He said, well we're having a meeting and if
you want to come, come on. That was obviously a challenge:
either join in the planning or shut up; if you're not going to do
anything, then don't complain. Maybe that's why.

KALAMU: So the march went on without the leaders?

KIINI: Yes. Isn't that dumb? I asked, who's going to make
the statement? Shawn said they gave it to the campus minister,
and he was going to do it.

So the march went downtown, and everything was cool
until they got to the capitol building, which is what had
happened the night before. There was no plan once they got to
the destination, and from there everything just went amok.
Based on what my girlfriend told me, the people who wanted
to be violent went one way, and the other people stayed at the
capitol building and tried to make themselves heard.

Now the people who wanted to be violent, they got beauty
salons, little corner stores, a Black Art gallery— when I say

197

Why L.A. Happened

"got" I mean they broke windows—they got Nation's Bank, Macy's. Then, since I was not there I can't say who looted Underground Atlanta, but of course it was probably either college students or young people who lived in Atlanta. They turned over some cars.

Eventually the group at the capitol dispersed. Two of the people who were in the planning meeting ended up talking with a person from SCLC. They told us the things that they had been advised to do. Most of those things were long term.

By the time Joel, Shawn and I got downtown, there wasn't a lot going on, but we did see the destruction that had been done. One sister I met was talking about how the police were going crazy and how the police had tried to beat her in the legs when she ran away. She said it was insane.

We left downtown and went back to the campus. The mayor came to campus under the pretense that he was coming to talk with us. He basically just made a speech saying don't do this and don't do that, and then he left. We had been told to gather in King's Chapel because the mayor was going to speak with us. When I hear "speak with us" I understand dialogue and communication. I don't understand that you're going to give us a speech.

Before he came to the chapel, he had a meeting with "the" student leaders who were really Morehouse SGA, Morehouse's "elected" leaders, and they really had nothing to do with the march or how it started. Only one person who was part of the planning meeting was there. Her name was Shawna, and she said they were changing everything around, no one up there had been involved in the march, and she didn't know what they were talking about.

After the mayor made his little speech, I went home. I said to myself, I did what needed to be done. The spark has been lit.

"It Was Either This Or Nothing."

These people can take it. I don't care. I was not about to fight Morehouse SGA to be heard. I guess that's something personal with me. If you want it that badly, go ahead, just so long something is being done. At that point I was surprised that anything was happening at all.

I went home and went back to school early in the morning on Friday. When I got to campus there were public service buses full of police in riot gear. Early in the morning they had set up around the perimeter of the campuses. They had surrounded all of the dorms. When I came out of my study abroad meeting, there were about four to six helicopters flying around. We stood out in the Spelman parking lot trying to decide what to do. Steve Bowser, the security person, told us to come inside the gates because the police were making arbitrary arrests, and we didn't want to be out in the streets.

Earlier that morning someone else had started another march. I know that Ast and Kmt, the African sisterhood and brotherhood at AUC, had planned a march, but I'm not sure that was the march that happened while I was in my meeting. Anyway, one of my friends who participated in that march said that they had security people, they were very organized. She said that the cops stopped them between Clark Courts, a residential area, and Clark's main campus and would not let them march any further. When they tried to return to campus, the cops prevented them from marching back. From what I understand, at that point when the cops wouldn't let them march downtown and wouldn't let them march back to campus, things quickly became chaotic. I don't know what the specific details were, but the cops and the students ended up fighting in the street. And then it got really crazy.

They broke into a Korean-owned liquor store. Most of us college students are under-aged, but that liquor store sold

199

alcohol to students, and in a sense that was biting the hand that feeds you. The day before they broke the window of the neighborhood grocery store. That was ridiculous. This is what distracts the public from the issue.

One person walked up to a photographer and broke a bottle over his head, and said, "put *this* on tv." They, of course, showed that on tv everywhere. They turned over and burned a car. Then the police came to push the demonstrators back. People started throwing things at the cops. The cops started firing tear gas. It was almost like combat. That's when the cops went on Morehouse's campus. They tear gassed Morehouse's campus. They tear gassed a dorm on Clark's campus. The police chief said they shot tear gas into the dorm because objects were being thrown at the police from the dorm, and tear gassing the dorm was the only way the police knew to stop the people who were throwing the objects. They even caught a security guard in uniform who was throwing rocks at the police.

At that point it was basically just combat. I decided I didn't want to be involved in that. Actually I was torn—I didn't want to be involved in a riot, but I did feel that if I wasn't there I wasn't doing anything to protest the verdict. Eventually I decided rioting was not a statement I cared to make.

As the tear gassing increased, people started dispersing. Then the police shut Clark, Morehouse and Spelman down. They blocked off the streets and wouldn't let anyone in or out. Eventually they allowed people to leave but only by car. You couldn't walk the streets. That was Friday, the last day. We had had a night and two days of active protest.

After the protests, people began to form organizing committees for long-range planning. I'm sort of removed from a lot of that because I live off campus. But I know that one of the committees dealt with economics, and their goal is when students return in the fall, they are going to organize a campaign to get the students to move their money from C&S and Wachovia to the Black-owned bank.

Once AUC finally got moving, it was time to go home.

KALAMU: About a month before Los Angeles you were in DC for a pro-choice demonstration—the largest demonstration in the history of the capitol. Was there as much coverage for the pro-choice demonstration as there was for the so-called Atlanta riots?

KIINI: Atlanta was international news. I hate to say it, but I really believe the reason was because Atlanta was violent. When I think about the fact that the pro-choice rally was basically ignored, it makes me analyze what this supposed democracy we are living in actually means. Obviously our voice is not counting. In the United States, either you're silent or you're violent, that's just the way it is.

I've heard a lot of people refer to this as a revolution, but to me it's not because the protests are over, and the power structure has not been changed.

KALAMU: I think you must make a distinction between random violent acts and confrontational acts. Having come through the civil rights movement, I can bear witness that a lot of what we did was confrontational, it was designed to interfere with the normal operations of the status quo and make it impossible for the status quo to continue going on, and at the same time the acts were designed to be non-violent in that offensive violence was not used as part of the confrontational tactic. I do think that in the context of where we are, as much as I disagree with non-violence as a philosophy, I do think it is important as a specific tactic, and it is important to learn when to use it and when not to use it. When you have numbers and you have an obvious, flagrant wrong that has been perpetrated, then a non-violent confrontational demonstration can be used. However, the issue is, are you dealing with confronting or disrupting the status quo?

KIINI: Yeah, I agree with that, and that's why we were demonstrating. We had to do something.

KALAMU: Anything else you want to say about what went on?

KIINI: Yes. MTV aired a session between Blacks and Koreans speaking to each other about what had happened. I thought it was necessary dialogue. But the general media focus on the conflict between Blacks and Asians resulted in taking the focus off of the white power structure and white people's role in causing the riots. At the end of the program the narrator said, we invited white people to come and speak, and they didn't come.

To me, that's a perfect example of race relations in America. Everyone is coming to the peace table saying, ok, let's work this out, but white people refuse to even come to the table. Generally speaking, white people don't acknowledge nor understand their role in our oppression, and when they do admit it, they are too defensive to discuss it. I really think more and more white people are seeing themselves as oppressors and are actually not being able to deal with that.

On the other hand, our anger at Koreans is extremely misdirected. We can't just look at Koreans and say, you have a business in our neighborhood, you're wrong for that, I'm angry with you. We need to look at why and how. I think part of Black people's problem right now is that there's no tangible, obvious goal. This may not be a revelation, but before people were saying, we want to ride on the front of the bus, we want to vote, we want this, that and the other. We have those things now.

There's nothing more that white people can do for us. To me, at this point, education is essential—and I don't mean public school or college. I really believe we need to stop focusing on white people. Not that the system is not to blame and the white people who run it should not be held accountable, but there's nothing more they can do for us. The rest of the work needs to be done ourselves.

That's it. You know, it all boils down to, a whole lot of people can articulate the problems, but the real question is what are the solutions, what are we going to do? That's what I'm trying to figure out.

KALAMU YA SALAAM is a professional editor/writer, producer and arts administrator. He is a senior partner in the public relations firm, Bright Moments (New Orleans), literary coordinator for the Contemporary Arts Center (New Orleans) and literary consultant to The National Black Arts Festival (Atlanta). Salaam is the editor of *WORD UP—Black Poetry Of The 80s From the Deep South* (1990) and leader of The Word Band poetry performance ensemble. *What Is Life?* will be released in 1993 by Third World Press.

We Who Believe in Freedom

Pearl Cleage

Last month, in the days following the Simi Valley verdict, I turned on my TV one afternoon to catch up on things in L.A. and thought I had fallen into a time warp as scenes of students demonstrating in and around campuses of the Atlanta University Center were flashed across the screen.

As a graduate of Spelman College and a participant in many campus demonstrations, both as a Spelman student and before that as a Howard University student, scenes of marching, chanting students made me feel nostalgic and hopeful. It is my belief that conscious African-American students ought to be in a constant rage and a constant search for ways to channel that rage into freedom struggle.

I was pleased to see these students participating in a proud legacy of protest. Glad to see Brother Mukasa still on the job as he was in 1969 when he came to speak at Yale while I was a student there for the summer and told me that I should probably sell my diamond engagement ring and buy some guns if I knew what was good for me and understood what America was all about.

Watching those students marching downtown the night the verdict was announced, I remembered many demonstrations, from the take-over of the Howard University administration building to protest the war in Vietnam and demand a redirection of the university's academic focus, to the intense

205

Why L. A. Happened

debates at Harkness Hall between the board of trustees at Morehouse College and a group of radical Black intellectuals—*teachers and students*—who had locked them in to facilitate their participation in the discussion.

I remembered when The Institute of the Black World opened on the corner of Chestnut and Beckwith streets and hosted such revolutionary scholars as C.L.R. James, Vincent Harding, Lerone Bennett Jr. and William Strickland, who spent hours engaged in discussions with passionate students who quoted Nkrumah and Karl Marx and Sonia Sanchez all in the same breath.

I remember the hastily organized teach-in after the killing of Black students during a protest at Jackson State, where participating faculty members made it clear to the protesting students that the whole point of their being in college was to learn enough to *do something,* and so even in the midst of protest they were expected to be reading and thinking and discussing and strategizing. Everyone agreed that knowledge was power, as were the pursuit of information, the struggle for analysis, the necessity for clarity.

But it quickly became clear to me that this was not 1967 or 1968 or 1971. These were students from a new generation with an anger and a frustration specific to them. And they were angry. At the verdict. At the police. At the violence. At their own feeling of helplessness and betrayal and vulnerability. They threw bottles and rocks and dodged tear gas and demanded meetings with high-level officials and ordered the police to leave their campuses.

They taunted and turned tail. They demanded justice, and they looted a liquor store. They appeared before us in all their contradictory young Blackness, and when the media arrived and the cameras turned in their direction, and the microphones were pointed and poised, the question was asked, as they must have known it would be: What do you want?

And the silence was deafening. *What did they want?* Did

they want to end the war in Vietnam? *It's over*. Did they want to demand Black studies in their classrooms? *They can major in Black studies if they want to do so*. Did they want an end to segregation in public facilities? *Done!* They were at a loss. They knew they were angry, but they weren't sure what they were angry about, other than the police coming on their campuses, and that couldn't be all it was since they were mad when the police got there.

What did they want? They wanted to be *included*. That's nothing to throw bottles about. City Hall is open every day. They wanted to be *considered*. No problem. Public meetings are announced in the paper every week so citizens can come and have their say. They wanted to *have a voice in things*. Great! Almost all of them are old enough to vote and to run for any office except president.

They wanted *Black businesses* on their campuses. Sounds like a job for some business students who want to get some experience before they graduate and open their own businesses in West End to help stimulate economic growth in the neighborhood and create jobs for their brothers and sisters.

So what's the problem? I felt like I was missing something. They were young and bright and literate, and they lived in a community that needs all their skills desperately. They were being trained to be the leaders and the strategists and the builders and the dreamers at the time when their people had never needed them more. And they were miserable. Miserable and *confused*. Because nobody will tell them the truth.

On the contrary. We spend inordinate amounts of time lying to them, these who represent our best and brightest and the best hope for whatever future we can squeeze out of this terrible place. We raised them to think that they can give to the world the best they have and that the best will come running back to them, regardless of race and class and gender. We've convinced them that the world is waiting for smart, creative, young Black people who have only to complete their college educations and the jobs will be offered, the book contracts will be signed, the deals will be done, and the paychecks will add up to $40,000 the first year out.

We've told them how different they are than their brothers and sisters living in misery just outside the gates surrounding their campuses. We've allowed them to use terms like *ghetto girl* and *project people* and didn't stop long enough to explain to them that this is unacceptable language with which to describe members of your extended family.

We have whipped them into a frenzy about the glories of the Olympics and the possibilities of corporate offices with a view of Stone Mountain and a box seat at the Super Bowl. We've ignored their angry rappers and their desperate movies and encouraged them to see themselves as *exceptions*. The ones who won't be ignored, brutalized, addicted, broken, beaten, raped, impregnated and abandoned. We've guided them into gilded cages and individual cocoons that seemed airless to them even as we extolled the virtues of that new BMW or that Caribbean vacation.

And now, as Brother Malcolm would say, the chickens have come home to roost. The beating of Rodney King and the verdict ripped away the mask we tried so hard to tie across their eyes, and they saw the America we had denied existed in all its brutal, videotaped glory. And they were surprised and scared and angry because we hadn't given them the tools to understand that for *oppressed* people, *freedom struggle is ongoing* and that the only real joy and happiness in life comes from passionate engagement with that collective struggle.

Confronting the GBI in the middle of Fair Street is a hard way to learn a lesson, and as a friend asked me long distance, *didn't they know this was America?* But better late than never. They probably would have come along a lot faster and been a lot more articulate when CNN stuck a microphone in their faces if we'd talked to them a little longer and told them the truth a little more, no matter how terrible we thought it was. *Nothing is more terrible than not knowing.*

But all that's water under the bridge now. Now at least America has shown us all where we stand, and *so be it.* The time for fantasies of individual salvation is past. We stand together or fall the same way. The police didn't ask Rodney King if he had graduated from Morehouse before they cracked his skull.

So welcome to the battle, young brothers and sisters. *We've been waiting for you.*

PEARL CLEAGE is a prolific writer who works in a variety of formats. She is the editor of *Catalyst* magazine and artistic director of Just Us Theater Company. Her plays include *puppetplay, Good News, Porch Songs, Banana Bread, Essentials* and *Hospice* (which won five AUDELCO awards for Outstanding Off-Broadway Achievement in 1982). Her poetry and short fiction collections include *Mad At Miles, The Brass Bed and Other Stories* (Third World Press), *One for the Brothers* and *We Don't Need No Music.* Her work has appeared in *Essence, Ms., Black Books Bulletin, The Journal of Negro Poetry* and *Negro Digest.*

part five . . .

STEPS TO START THE DREAMS

The Lesson of Rodney King

Michael Bradley

As of this writing (April 30, 1992), North American newspapers carry banner headlines about the riots in Los Angeles resulting from the verdict in the Rodney King affair. (Rodney King was the Black L.A. motorist who was brutally beaten by four white policemen on March 3, 1991.) Unlike many similar incidents in the United States (and Canada), the torment of Rodney King was not just another "allegation" lacking objective and dramatic proof; the police brutality was videotaped by an amateur cameraman, and the tape was broadcast throughout the world. From the evidence of this tape, prosecutors in the trial of the accused policemen counted 56 blows and kicks delivered by the four white policemen on a helpless and writhing Rodney King during the course of an 81-second beating that was obviously, to any objective person, "excessive use of force." Indeed, anyone watching that videotape—and it required a strong stomach to view it completely—could not but conclude that the four white policemen were simply indulging in a spasm of pure racial hatred and violence.

Because it had been videotaped, however, this particular

incident could not be ignored and covered up. The four white policemen were charged with multiple counts of brutality and brought to trial. Perhaps inevitably, the white-wash mechanisms began to operate almost immediately; *there was not one Black on the jury* even though, given the demographics of Los Angeles, three or four Blacks would have been fair racial representation. Presumably, it was considered that Blacks would be biased against the white police defendants. An Asian American and a Hispanic American were the minorities who could be easily intimidated by the remaining 10 white members of this jury.

Nevertheless, even with the racially skewed jury, many North Americans thought that justice would prevail *this* time if only because the evidence was so obvious and unarguable.

Incredibly, the jury acquitted the four policemen on charges of using "excessive force" (definitely an euphemism in this case). Even the state prosecutors were amazed at the jury's verdict. Black community leaders were, perhaps, not so amazed: "If something in you can die, that something died," said Rev. Cecil Murray of the African Methodist Episcopal Church in South Central Los Angeles. Watching the news coverage of the verdict on television in his church packed with fellow viewers, Murray fought back tears and declared the verdict a tragedy—"Not because it's unbelievable but because it is believable." In fairness, it should be added that many white residents of L.A. were equally outraged. One of them, Rose Brown, who drove to the courthouse to hear the expected guilty verdict was interviewed by the *Los Angeles Times:* "I'm not only shocked," she said, "but I'm hurt for Americans as a people. I don't think Rodney King was on trial but America was on trial."

But other whites, and probably a secret majority of them, applauded the acquittal of the four cops. "I'm glad they got off," Barbara Williams told the *Los Angeles Times*. "They did what they were trained to do."

213

Why L.A. Happened

Incredibly, Black community leaders in Los Angeles pleaded for calm and non-violence. But it was a vain appeal, understandably. Rage boiled over at the patent injustice of the so-called justice system, and infuriated Blacks took to the streets to dish out to the white motorists a dose of what Rodney King had taken. Looters ravaged stores, motorists were dragged from their cars and pummeled, and demonstrators rushed local police headquarters. Some 51 people were killed, 2,383 injured; a state of emergency was declared by Mayor Tom Bradley; the National Guard was deployed by Governor Pete Wilson. Such is the human tragedy when justice is perverted and denied. The ongoing cost will be that Rodney King will not be forgotten for a long, long time, and if I were a white cop or just a white resident of L.A., I would be very nervous for a long, long time. Justifiably nervous. Guiltily nervous. When justice fails, vengeance is the only, and inevitable, recourse of the disenfranchised.

This entire incident is just one more in a long and depressing chronicle of racism and injustice perpetuated by the Western World, and so-called "Western civilization," upon non-whites. It is just one more in a series of *judicial* injustices committed against non-whites since the belated Emancipation Proclamation. The technical, judicial injustice applied to the Rodney King issue is a lingering shadow of 550 years of "believable" inhumanity practiced upon non-whites by the Western Civilization of Europeans and North Americans. Before the Simi Valley verdict of April 29, 1992, there had been 425 years of absolute slavery of a savagery unknown elsewhere in the world, followed by a century of semi-serfdom and racial denigration after the official end of slavery in America, continued by almost three more decades of racial discrimination in housing, education, employment, health care. The riots in Los Angeles which followed the jury's incredible acquittal did not result only from this particular legal case. The *judicial* injustice was the last straw in *five and a half centuries of obscene inhumanity.* The race riots that shocked America were a natural and inevitable response to the technical and judicial injustice thought (hopefully) to be ended by a videotape, so that true *social justice* could begin. But the White Establishment sought, once more, to peg its hopes on a technical and judicial injustice. As far as American "Mainstream/Middle Class/White" society is concerned, well, it may go down in history as the *last* racial injustice they enjoyed.

Consider, for example, that every single juror *swore on the Bible* to be impartial in the pursuit of justice based solely upon the evidence. Each juror, in effect, made a covenant with God to mete out justice based on the truth. This covenant has disturbing implications for non-whites all over the world, *and particularly for Blacks in North America*, because it involves a terrible historical irony.

Traditionally, African society was so remarkably non-violent and crime-free that there was not even a (West) African word for "jail." Indeed, this peace and general harmony of African societies amazed and awed early Euro-Arabic travellers south of the Sahara. Ibn Batuta, an Arab explorer, first published his *Travels in Asia and Africa* in Morocco in 1356. About Black African countries, he wrote the following:

> They are seldom unjust and have a greater abhorrence of injustice than any other people. Their sultan shows no mercy to anyone who is found guilty of the least act of it. There is complete security in the country. Neither traveller nor inhabitant in it has anything to fear from robbers or men of violence. They do not confiscate the property of any white man who dies in their country, even if it be uncounted wealth. On the contrary, they give it into the charge of some trustworthy person among the whites, if such can be found, until the rightful heir takes possession of it. (Taken from Basil Davidson's *Lost Cities of Africa*, pg. 79, translated into English by H.A.R. Gibb, 1929.)

Why L.A. Happened

Ibn Batuta's account may be somewhat exaggerated and romanticized, and if so, it is probably due to his cultural shock at experiencing the African concept of social harmony. Ibn Batuta had travelled widely throughout the known world accessible to Arabs of his day, from Morocco, throughout the Middle East and Central Asia, and on to China and Indo-China. He had a broad grasp of various peoples and cultures of his time from 20 years of first-hand experience. If he wrote about the Africans in this way, there must have been more than a grain of truth to it. Elsewhere he states (as did other early travellers) that there was no (repeat, *no*) racial discrimination among the Black Africans.

The Black African concept of the way things should be was a harmony of past-present-future life welded together wholistically by a compassionate religion and social structure (as human cultures go). When Black Africans were torn from their traditional cultural and religious fabric by the European slave trade of 1444-1820, and when unfortunates from various parts of Africa were thrown together as anonymous slaves to their own bewilderment and confusion, they desperately sought some compassionate and unifying spiritual force that could make a brutal existence endurable.

In one of history's cruelest ironies, they embraced their masters' religion, Christianity, as the only common creed available to them. And, in *all* cases, they embraced it with a fervor that generally amused whites (since whites did not share and may not be capable of sharing spiritual ecstasy, except for a few extraordinary individuals), while in *most* cases they seriously accepted the compassionate words attributed to Jesus at face value (which their masters did not) because they saw an apparent sameness between Christ's injunctions and the traditional social harmony they had known, and lost.

In their despair, they also equated the Jews' captivity in Egypt as paralleling their own enslavement in the New World.

Few of the African slaves could read or had any grasp of

European historical reality. They could not be expected to know that the entire context of both the Old Testament and New Testament was really as un-African as it is possible to imagine. Even after Emancipation in the United States, and even after some Blacks had achieved reasonable education, that African capacity for fervor and almost metabolic African need for social harmony and compassion blinded many Blacks as to the real nature of Western Man's psychology *and blinded them to the fact that the various "white man's religions," deep down, simply reflected this violent and chauvinistic psyche.*

For the fact of the matter is that the Old Testament and the New Testament—that Holy Bible upon which the Los Angeles jurors swore—is, *if it is considered* objectively, one of the most ethno-centric, anti-feminist, potentially racist and certainly violent documents ever penned by any group of humanity. The Holy Bible is, essentially, the saga of a uniquely wrathful and decidedly uncompassionate god who made a covenant with just one small tribe, the Hebrews, that they are the universe's "Chosen People." You will look in vain for such arrogance, absurdity and *injustice* among the writings of Buddhism, Hinduism, Shinto, Taoism; you will look in vain for anything similar among the advanced African religions, of the Yoruba and Akan, that European slavery disconnected from Africans brought to the Americas. None of these non-white religions are nearly so racist, ethno-centric, anti-feminist and pathologically violent as the three Western religions (Judaism, Christianity and Islam) which all "devolved" from the *Old Testament* and the wrathful god of the Chosen People.

This truth is slowly percolating up to African Americans and even invading the ivied halls of institutions like Yale Divinity School. On April 24-25, 1992, I was invited to participate in a symposium called "Racism: A Crisis of the Heart" at Yale Divinity School in New Haven, Connecticut. At that symposium, I presented the gist of *The Iceman Inheritance* and *Chosen People From The Caucasus*: that Western Man is basically more violent than other human groups because of significant Neanderthal ancestry; that racism, sexism, ethnocentrism and inordinate technological "progress" are all symptoms of this basic Neanderthal mind-set; that the ancient Hebrews originated in a region of known Neanderthal concentration; the god and religion conceived by these early migrants into Palestine merely (naturally) reflected their own psychology. Christianity, as an offshoot of Judaism, like Islam, inherently retains much of the original ethnocentricity, anti-feminism and inhumanity ("believe in *me* or else") of that early Hebrew conception.

The focus of the Yale symposium was the fervent, but unfounded, assumption by African-American clerics that Christianity was the only religion capable of defeating racism throughout the world; they held the symposium to develop ideas on strategy. But, in my view, which I tried to defend with actual evidence, not hopeful belief, was that Christianity is *and always was*, fundamentally racist, ethno-centric, anti-feminist and that the god of the *New Testament*, while not as violent as the god of the *Old Testament*, contained plenty of "believe in me or be damned" intolerance and *inhumanity*. Other major religions of the world, and traditional African ones, simply do not incorporate or embrace "exclusive/chauvinist" and "violence" to any comparable degree. *They* (pick any one), *not Christianity*, are better conceptual/spiritual orientations for combatting racism and could be embraced with fervor by African Americans to better effect.

This view was, of course, a "heresy" in the eyes of the traditionalist, fundamentalist African-American Christians in the audience—and there were a number who were shocked.

However, there were also a number of younger "Christian" seminarians, some studying at Yale and some who had come to the symposium from other divinity schools, who were not so shocked. They had come to the same conclusion, but on spiritual and simple observational grounds. They welcomed a presentation of the biological and anthropological "proof."

The major, hurtful lesson for African Americans in the Rodney King affair is not simply that white society, and white police who protect it, are needlessly brutal because of Neanderthal ancestry—I think that most progressive Blacks know that they live in a "culture of violence" (as Penny Hess depicts Western Civilization in her book of the same title)—but an even worse realization: that even the spiritual, religious and judicial concepts of white society, all originally articulated in basic form in the *Old Testament*, are fundamentally "against" and unsuited to African-American human rights and aspirations. Those jurors swore on the Bible, but it is a white covenant...and it always was.

The too-believable injustices of the Rodney King affair has angered me so much that I cannot help but make a plea: African Americans must forsake the white man's social structures, concepts of justice and, yes, even religion and return, as far as possible, to genuine African values and identity (insofar as these can be accurately recovered and reconstructed). I make this plea, not only for you who are Black, but for myself (and my son, and other people) *who are white*. Some of us realize that we are all living in a culture of violence, and we would prefer an alternative; some of us have fought, thought and written in the hope of attaining an alternative. We are "white," but non-whites. All non-whites, including Asian Americans and Hispanic Americans of mixed Spanish/Black/Amerindian origins must strive to create some cultural alternative to the Western World's culture of violence that came from the Caucasus so long ago.

There are 30-40 million Blacks in North America, and a return to traditional African values by so many could not be thwarted, defeated or eradicated by white supremacy. An unassailable cultural alternative would be created, and many non-Blacks would probably find greater security and compassion for their own values than anyone might suspect. African

219

Why L.A. Happened

Americans have more allies than are evident from the Rodney King injustice, and we continue to look to Blacks to create an alternative to our culture of violence.

NOTES

All information and quotes concerning the Rodney King affair have been taken from the *Toronto Sun's* coverage (April 30, 1992, page 1 and 2 based on *Los Angeles Daily News* reports, plus Reuters and UPI wire services) and the *Toronto Star* (April 30, 1992, page 1 and A18 based on *Los Angeles Times* coverage and Reuter/AP wire services).

MICHAEL BRADLEY is the author of *The Iceman Inheritance* and *The Columbus Conspiracy: The Black Discovery of America.* "The Lesson of Rodney King" is excerpted from *Chosen People From the Caucasus: Jewish Origins, Delusions, Deceptions and Historical Role in the Slave Trade, Genocide and Cultural Colonization* (Third World Press, 1992).

From These Black and Brown Streets:

L.A. Revisited

Luis J. Rodriguez

"Go ahead and kill us, we're already dead...."
—Young participant in the 1992 Los Angeles
uprising as quoted in *USA Today*, 5/1/92.

From Chicago, I watched the fires that consumed miles of
Los Angeles beginning on April 29, the day a jury in Simi
Valley declared four police officers innocent of excessive force
against Rodney King.

Fire for me has been a constant metaphor, the squeeze of
memory against the backdrop of inner city reality. You see,
South Central Los Angeles was once home. I was 11 years-old
when the 1965 Watts uprising tore through my old neighborhood. In 1970, at age 16, I was beaten and arrested during the
Chicano Moratorium Against the War—the so-called East L.A.
Riot—which exploded when sheriff's officers and police attacked demonstrators, leaving at least three dead and much of
Whittier Boulevard in flames.

So watching L.A. burn again was nothing new nor
surprising. Yet, the spray of TV images and the reportage that

Why L.A. Happened

followed the violence failed to jibe with the reality on the streets or with what I knew.

To me, the L.A. uprising wasn't about blind rage. It wasn't about "race" or "crime"—America's twin fears. It wasn't even just about Rodney King.

The heart of the 1992 Los Angeles uprising remained in the African-American community. But this was not Watts 1965. This time a significant number of Latinos—who make up almost half of South Central's population—were heavily involved. Latinos, whites and Asians from Fairfax, Westwood and parts of the San Fernando Valley also took part. In cities across the country, all kinds of people led protests against the verdict—an issue which, according to polls and interviews, more Americans agree with regardless of color.

A critical unity was informally forged by the two most exploited and oppressed communities in L.A.: African American and Latino. This is an important challenge to the power structure in that city. In fact, Koreatown, portrayed in the news as a key "victim" of the rage, is 70% Latino (most Korean business owners, as in South Central, do not live there).

A couple of weeks after the unrest, I went back to Los Angeles and traveled through the stricken areas, watching mothers walk by curled steel from caved-in structures and children run pass boarded up windows. A Salvadoran peddler told me her fellow peddlers, Salvadoran and Mexican, have been terrorized and deported since the unrest, many of them losing their products at the hands of the government ("Isn't this stealing?" she asked.) And a South Central mother from the Nickerson Gardens housing project said she was tired of having the whole country turn against her community. Why, she wanted to know, are the African and Latino communities paying the price when so many others were involved?

It's time to set the record straight. It's time to tell the truth of the L.A. uprising, one of the most important events of the century, yet the most confused and misconstrued in recent memory.

L.A.'s violence was the first major social response to an economic revolution which began years ago. This country has been undergoing a shift from an industrial-based energy system to one based on electronics. Computers and robotics are producing more commodities with less people. Instead of opening up the vast resources and collective intelligence to provide for all, these developments are hampered by production relations based on profits, throwing more and more people into the streets.

Today, almost a quarter of the American population lives below the poverty level: millions of people cannot obtain their basic necessities of life. L.A. alone lost some 100,000 jobs in the last decade (it has now the second largest homeless population in the country). Many of these shuttered factories—such as Goodyear Tire, General Motors and Bethlehem Steel—were based in the South Central area. The great abundance in most cities is largely inaccessible to most people because the distribution of society's goods is subject to those who can best afford them—not to those who most need them.

I saw one TV image of two mothers, Black and Brown, putting shoes on their children in the midst of a smoldering ruin. I don't consider this "criminal" activity—not when their livelihoods have been systematically "looted" all these years. Thus, the taking of commodities during the L.A. uprising is a natural means of "circulating" commodities that have long been denied them by the mode of distribution.

And this is not limited to people of color. A friend related to me about a recent trip to eastern Ohio, coal country, which has seen thousands of jobs disappear and cuts in general assistance programs. Some of the disenfranchised white youth asked him: "How do we have a rebellion like in L.A.?"

At the same time, those in the highest levels of power in

Why L.A. Happened

America—whom I consider the real criminals—have enriched themselves with corporate bail-outs and tax breaks. It's evident the government only exists to insure that the top 1% of the population continues to reap more than 60% of the country's wealth.

Instead of giving back what it has taken, the government's response to L.A.—a united front from Mayor Bradley to Governor Wilson to President Bush—was to send in troops against the people. On national TV, Bush called the city's rage "the brutality of a mob." He also labelled Saddam Hussein, Manuel Noriega and Libya's Ghadafy as "outlaws" before militarily attacking them. A little more than a year ago, the U.S. armed forces were in the Persian Gulf—now a section of them were in Los Angeles, killing members of our community!

A reign of terror has been instituted in Los Angeles. Efforts by the Crips and Bloods to unite (and to stop a bloody warfare which has claimed hundreds of lives over the last 10 years) have been met by police raids and arrests, by "mysterious" drive-bys and media lies.

Hundreds of Latinos are also being pulled from their homes and jobs and deported without due process of law. Children are now missing, and nobody knows whether they are in Tuijuana or dead. The repression which the people of South Central and Pico-Union have long experienced is now official.

It's proof that any serious challenge to the economic and political underpinnings of poverty in this country will be dealt with swiftly. This is the foundation for Bush's "New World Order" (words last uttered by Adolph Hitler), and this is an outrage.

The Los Angeles violence was far from random, far from malicious. Many markets, banks and liquor stores were struck in a swathe that cut all the way up to Hollywood. Koreatown took a beating because of what it has represented: exploitative prices and the general mistreatment of African-American and

Latino customers. (I know—I've been followed, told to hurry if I linger too long and then threatened with police action if I so much as argue.) It was not against Koreans per se, as the media portrayed this; it was against exploitation.

The uprising implicitly, if not explicitly, attacked the class nature of the system—a system which can no longer provide for its people and which must be reorganized around the new tools of production.

In fact, the recent proposal by the Bloods and Crips for rebuilding the city is not about bringing back the burned-out businesses (as the city aims to do)—the community doesn't need any more furniture or liquor stores!

They are calling for a new Los Angeles. They are calling for every abandoned building to be gutted, for new parks and community centers to be built, for the re-pavement of streets and sidewalks. They are demanding increased lighting and more trees, for businesses which have a stake in the community, for the reconstruction of schools and more books. They are calling for jobs which pay decent and livable wages—not the low-paying jobs they are often offered, if any.

And the total cost of the Crips/Bloods package is estimated at $3.726 billion—far less than the $500 billion used to bail out the Savings and Loans!

At the end of the proposal were the words: "Give us the hammer and the nails, we will rebuild the city."

We have now closed a period of development in this country and entered another one. The polarity between wealth and poverty is increasing and changing the temper of our times. Though words like "race," "riot" and "lawlessness" are thrown about, they don't mean the same thing today.

The relative prosperity in the country that marked the period during the Watts uprising is over. Then, the government was able to infuse the community with billions of dollars. Allocations of federal funds grew from some $10 million prior to the rebellion to about $5 billion in 1967. Although nothing significant changed in Watts, they can't even do this today.

Additionally, police power in Los Angeles has become more sophisticated, more intense. In 1965, the LAPD instituted the nightly eye-in-the-sky helicopter probes that continue to this day. They built a computerized system in the basement of Parker Center which details every street, every alley, almost every nook and cranny in Los Angeles, for quick and efficient deployment of force. The aim: no more Watts rebellions.

Suddenly, drugs appeared on the scene on a vast scale. A long-time Watts resident once told me, "downers were standing up on every street corner after Watts." Heroin, PCP and later crack moved through South Central in successive stages.

I also recall, before Watts exploded, that there was a low level of gang activity. There were groups such as the Slausons, the Gladiators and Bishops. But they weren't as organized nor as long-standing as those in the barrios of the Mexican community—some which originated in the 1920s. Then, by the early 1970s, there were skirmishes involving a group called the Crips. I know—I was a member of a gang in the San Gabriel Valley at the same time. In the jails and youth detention centers, we all knew about the various Crips formations. The Bloods soon followed as an amalgamation of groups, such as the Brims and Pirus.

In the 1980s, this flowering would make Los Angeles the so-called gang capital of the world. But this never came from the youth; it arose outside their communities.

This is why during a number of recent unity meetings, former enemies embraced with tears in their eyes while tying the red and blue bandannas together. And they questioned: who made us kill one another? Who indeed!

Since 1965, police abuse cases escalated, some went to court—but still no justice. I myself participated in organizations surrounding the deaths of Danny Garcia, Randell Miles and a few others killed by LAPD or sheriff's deputies. I myself had four of my closest friends killed by law enforcement officers before I turned 18. And beside the beating I sustained during the Chicano Moratorium, I also suffered other attacks, including a 1973 arrest for allegedly assaulting a peace officer after being jumped by eight sheriff's deputies one night in the parking lot of an after-hours club in Norwalk (another time, another story).

Over the years, there developed a tightening of the police state in Los Angeles. The LAPD has been neither beholden nor accountable to any elected representatives or city officials. There has been no "public power" capable of curtailing the police. They run their department with impunity, holding the power of life and death over our communities.

Over the years, several groups tried to initiate a civilian review board, without great success. Eventually the community obtained an injunction against the use of the deadly choke hold, a leading killer of African-American males (although Chief Daryl Gates claimed Blacks were more susceptible to the hold because of their anatomically different windpipes!).

Instances of police brutality became full-fledged police terror—a systematic, orchestrated pattern of control. The LAPD's "Operation Hammer," with the use of an armored battering ram, resulted in the rounding up and detention of thousands of South Central youth. By the time Rodney King was stomped on by Foothill division police and captured on videotape, so many people, mostly African-American and Latino, had already been killed.

For instance, during the Rodney King brutality trial, the *Los Angeles Daily News* reported that 57 unarmed citizens, mostly of color, had been killed by the Los Angeles County sheriff's department in 1991. Four of the cases were brought to civil suit—and were lost. Latasha Harlins, a 15 year-old African American, was shot in the back after an argument with a Korean store owner over orange juice. This was also on videotape—but the store owner received only five years probation!

Why L.A. Happened

The acquittals of the police officers who brutalized Rodney King were only the tip of a mountain of unjust verdicts.

This was the stage that preceded the 1992 Los Angeles uprising. If we are to understand the implications of what happened in Los Angeles, we have to look closely at these and other critical issues representative of a new era of change—including great possibility—in this country. There just won't be any peace—in spite of all the armies, all propaganda, all the code words to the contrary—until those possibilities are accessible to all, until we take back the fruit from the efforts of our own hands.

In every major city in America—in my current home town of Chicago where a number of police torture cases and killings have long been documented—there are daily "quiet riots" going on, ready to explode on the street. This is not a warning, it's a fact of life.

LUIS J. RODRIGUEZ is an award-winning poet, journalist and critic whose works have appeared in *The Nation*, *Chicago Reporter*, *Playboy* and *Los Angeles Weekly*, among others. He is also the publisher of the Tia Chucha Press, which has published poetry by African-American, Puerto-Rican, Chicano and Native-American writers. A book about growing up in Watts and the East Los Angeles area (*Always Running: A Memoir of La Vida Loca*) is scheduled for publication in the fall of 1992 by Curbstone Press.

South Central: Some Reflections

Mari Evans

Our initial Black/White encounter was adversarial: we continued as combatants—physically and psychologically engaged in a grotesque pas de deux—Freedom involuntarily paired with Oppression, a deadly dueling, diametric in direction and intent; opponents who, after over 400 years of rancorous combat still inhabit overlapping worlds, worlds as specific and discrete as the black and white that distinguishes the dancers.

Until the exercise of power is mutual, until experiencing oneself fully—competent, empowered, whole—can be enjoyed and shared by more than the select, the privileged, what illogic to expect either dancer to be indifferent or untouched by contemporary circumstances, dumb to ancestral rhythms, to live harmoniously with the opponent, or to 'love' beyond any pretense.

The oppressed, and we are oppressed, are crisis-oriented. We can summon a great cohesiveness in times of extreme sadness or joy. Or trouble. For it is then that we understand on an acutely self-conscious level, our national 'family-hood.' We respond to an understood, unstated mandate, and we move from the very edges of nowhere to come together toward one end: To make, according to our various instincts and experiences, the necessary statement.

This is what happened in South Central Los Angeles. One mind—a single thought expressed a thousand ways; one heart—beating to multitudinous rhythms; one image—flaming a million eyes; one voice choked with the family's rage.

We are a mystical people, moving instinctively when the drums announce danger. Or dance. And we appear, magically, without announcement or arrangement, in the same place at the same time, charged by the same impulse. In-bond. We come, each bringing part of what is needed: Bullets, bandages, or more simply, bodies. Further, and contrary to all allegation, it is a compulsive, self-less comingtogetherness: The sound above sound above sound. And what South Central heard, in the wake of the drum-roll, was a call to war: Two armies, each diverse, the State—structured as usual; the People—ad hoc as usual, enemies who share a history, who know each other well; opposed to each other in spirit, conviction and intent, psychologically anxious and physically ready for confrontation: They had no option but to contend. And South Central was, in the truest sense, a battle of no mean significance in the ongoing war between the State and the People.

The notion for contraband, therefore, was never the motivating force in South Central—it was rage, accumulative and catalytic, careening through the minds and the bodies of the oppressed, a focused fury, wild and empowering that pulsed the firestorm that swept and destroyed sections of Los Angeles. The *notion* for contraband—mere martial music heard from a distance; an addenda, the recall of classic privilege, the exercise of a traditional 'right': The devaluing of that closest to the enemy's heart; a violent sharing and abuse of what he treasures.

In South Central the spoils of war were stated crudely in the direct language of the oppressed and with an honesty that could only be offensive in its blunt immediacy. For, after all, the only appropriate spoils of war, that is, those understood, endorsed and sanctioned by The Fathers of the World, are expressed in terms of oil, or minerals, or diamonds, or a country's cultural artifacts and treasures. Or land. A 'taking' that to satisfy propriety must be preceded by an acceptable statement of mission, such as "...to bring democracy." Or God.

The incredible "Why?" which seemed to surround South Central was purely rhetorical, of course. Any child who has observed the 'haves' and 'have nots' knows "why." Obviously, however, some of the affluent, highly visible folk who converged on South Central to arrange public forums during which the insurrectionists might exchange views with each other, learn how irrational they had been and even, possibly, begin to learn to love each other—obviously these well-intentioned folk could not recall that the issue was about control, and about power, and powerlessness. That's *why*. And what's love got to do with it?

Certainly an oppressive society knows "why." Frantz Fanon (1968) probably said it best: "In fact, the settler is right when he speaks of knowing "them" well, for it is the settler who has brought the native into existence and who perpetuates his existence." So, yes. The national White viewing public traversing the nation's expressways and avoiding the South Centrals of the land, knew "why," for either passively or aggressively they had helped bring the "South Central's" into being. And, Forever CIAman Bush was clearly thinking-on-his-feet when he did not bother to rush from Pennsylvania Avenue to the smoke of the battleground. He, too, knew "why," for as a major player his staffing, nominations, reversals, vetoes and cutbacks had been crucial in molding and shaping the conditions that festered and smouldered in South Central and made of it a laboratory waiting to explode.

Therefore, in the shock-generated comingtogether that occurred in South Central following the brazen "no-fault" acquittal of four white policemen for the murderous attack on

Why L.A. Happened

Rodney King, a visible member of 'them,' the *thought* was the impulse, the *thing*, and the possibility of personal danger only a ripple on the fringes of the mind. As to the contraband? Armies have always looted and raped: Ask the Europeans. Ask the Americans. Are not these 'traditional' components of war, and is not the larger concept of war itself, that is, the need to control or kill pitted against the human determination to resist or die—the real horror?

South Central heard the drums and responded appropriately—if, that is, one can acknowledge oppression as an ongoing experience for African Americans; can admit to an escalating climate of brutality and confrontation—ultimate in its intensity, and if one can agree that the larger violence—that propounded by the State, overshadows the lesser violence of rage expressed through civil unrest, which is the recurrent response of the oppressed and nominally powerless.

None of the bemused questions regarding South Central were valid; answers stumbled, screamed and stared their way into the consciousness if allowed. And there remain no legitimate "why's." The only unknowns that linger, stalking the periphery, are these: "Where next? How soon? and Over what?" Their long shadows almost obscure the immediate future since no one expects the massive intellectual, socio-economic and political changes that *must* occur to occur any time soon.

I would argue that while my generation, building on the impressive achievements of our ancestors, changed the tenor of battle significantly, neither we, nor those immediately after, seem to have made the number of successful strikes we thought we were making. A period of regressive political behavior and apathy ensued. Unfortunately, our children and others—some less politically able, some less politically committed, but many secure, stalwart and courageous have inherited the struggle. It is not finished; it is not over. The bells of injustice continue to ring and the drums of resistance continue to sound.

The challenge is to be hardworking and constant. Fearless. Having understood the bells *and* the drums, more Kenneths and Glorias, more Keishas and Antwans, more Nzingas and Cinques, moving to the sound above sound above sound—join the ranks each daybreak. We are all in this together, and have been—but now we seem to know it.

As a family/Nation, focused and committed, we have no option but to be analytical, prepared and creative as we meet the enemy in every conceivable arena, on every imaginable battlefront, fitting strategy to situation. It won't be over until we say it's over. And we will not say it's over until Justice prevails, until opportunity for the least of us is secured, until strong, healthy, confident Black women and men stride purposefully through the land, and the children run free with their joyous African selves.

We understand South Central perfectly. This, therefore, is a statement of mission, clear and unconfuted: A Luta Continua.

MARI EVANS, educator, writer, activist, resides in Indianapolis. She is the author of numerous articles, several children's books, performed theater pieces, two musicals and four volumes of poetry. Her most recent, *A Dark and Splendid Mass*, will be released Fall 1992 by Harlem River Press. She edited the highly acclaimed *Black Women Writers (1950-1980): A Critical Evaluation*. Her work has been widely anthologized in collections and text books.

part six . . .

FROM THE HARD HEART

TIM JACKSON is an illustrator and designer. His political and satirical cartoons have appeared in newspapers across the country. Jackson's Creative License Studio is based in Chicago.

This Is America

Terry McMillan

I remember when I first saw that videotape. I wanted to hide my face but I couldn't. I thought for sure it was shot in South Africa, but no, the newscaster said Los Angeles. And it was 1991. The cops were kicking Rodney King as if he were a dog who'd bitten them, beating him with their billy clubs as he lay curled up on the pavement. They clubbed him 56 times.

In the following weeks I, like millions of others, watched the tape over and over, feeling more enraged each time. "They'll go to jail," is what my friends and I kept saying. "It's an open-and-shut case. It's in living color." The evidence of police brutality was indisputable; we were certain that for once the police would be held accountable. Guilt for them would finally be inescapable. Hah!

On Wednesday night, I was at a barbecue at my white neighbor's home. When I got home, I put my son to bed. An hour later, my sister knocked on the door. "I guess you heard about Rodney?" she said. And I said no, the news wasn't even on yet. She told me that the jury in Simi Valley, a mostly white suburb of Los Angeles, had acquitted the four policemen on all counts, with the exception of one officer, who'd been tried for one count of assault. I felt ill. Then the phone started ringing.

Why L.A. Happened

When the verdict from the all-white jury finally came on the news—after a seismologist had gone on and on about earthquakes and aftershocks and faults—I sat on the floor, dazed. I mean, 20 years ago I lived in Los Angeles when it was a clean, safe, relatively boring place. And then I remembered when the police started flying over homes in South Central Los Angeles in helicopters and how it seemed as if overnight L.A. had become a police state, at least where Blacks and Hispanics lived. I never saw a police helicopter fly over Beverly Hills or Malibu.

It breaks my heart to know that President Bush thinks America is still such a great place for *everybody*. It angers me when I'm told to put my hand over my chest to say the Pledge of Allegiance, to sing "God Bless America" when I see this kind of flagrant racism and am asked to accept it.

I'm mad. Everybody should be mad. How did this trial ever manage to take place before a jury with no Blacks? And, despite this, why were the jurors unable to see right from wrong? Don't white folks believe in God? Don't they believe in justice? After all, they're the ones who created the Constitution and the Bill of Rights.

The jury based its verdict on what Rodney King purportedly did before the 81-second video was shot. What could one man do to four men armed with guns and clubs that would merit this kind of violence?

Watching the fires burning on TV, I understood immediately why people resort to violence. When you feel helpless and angry and there's nowhere to turn for help, you strike out at anybody. Mayor Tom Bradley can't do anything but beg, and no one's interested in listening to him. I'm not.

I lived in Arizona for three years and hated it not only because we could not get Martin Luther King's birthday made into a holiday, but because the white folks were happy about their power over what happened there—they felt triumphant.

In my mind, there's no greater crime than overt injustice.

This one was in color. When four officers go free, when Mike Tyson goes to prison and William Kennedy Smith doesn't, when Clarence Thomas is appointed to the Supreme Court to make a point about justice, I am reminded that America remains a racist and perverse place to live.

And when you are fortunate enough to live in a pretty neighborhood, pay your bills on time and write books that people read, people think you can be shielded from the harsh realities of this nature. Well, I'm not that shielded. And millions in this country aren't either.

My brother is in prison right now. He was arrested 10 miles from Simi Valley for drunk driving. Fortunately, he didn't get beaten. How many white men have gone to jail for the same offense? How many innocent Black men who have been beaten never made it on videotape? And now, what difference would it make?

I have never trusted policemen, even the smiling ones. That badge stands more for badgering than safety, and the power it confers has forever gone to some of their heads. When you give men power, they usually abuse it, and this incident is no exception.

The humiliation and outrage that Americans—whites and Blacks, people of color alike—feel is valid. We're entitled to it, and now the focus is on our anger and not on the injustice itself.

This is America. The land of the free. Home of the brave. Well, I'm not buying into it today. I do not believe in violence. But if we have to do what we did in Watts in 1965 to let the Los Angeles Police Department, the city and the Government know that we're not going to tolerate this kind of travesty, then I say we have to make our point any way we can.

I really don't want to see innocent people hurt; already too many have died, many more Blacks than whites. As African Americans, we don't have that much as it is, and when we burn and kill, it's usually in our own backyard. I hope we don't do that.

Why L.A. Happened

It's unfortunate that this case, as an acquittal, can never be appealed. I wonder how Rodney King is feeling. I wonder if the jurors would feel differently if he had been their son.

My brother should be back at work. Those jurors should be forced to know what it feels like to be kicked and hit with a baton while lying on concrete. And those policemen should've been behind bars a long time ago. Praying for guidance. Something. A conscience maybe.

"This Is America" was first printed as an Op-Ed in the May 1, 1992 issue of the New York Times *(©1992), which is distributed by The New York Times Special Features.*

TERRY MCMILLAN is the author of *Waiting to Exhale, Disappearing Acts* and *Mama*, and editor of *Breaking Ice*, an anthology of contemporary African-American fiction. She has been a fellow at both Yaddo and the MacDowell Colony. She has received grants from the PEN American Center, the Authors League, the Carnegie Fund, the New York Foundation for the Arts and the National Endowment for the Arts. She is currently teaching creative writing at the University of Arizona (Tucson).

Let Freedom Ring

bell hooks

When the verdict in the Rodney King case was announced, I was in Holland where I had come to teach and live
for several months. Having studied the country before I arrived,
I knew that it had a large Black population made up of
immigrants and Dutch-born descendants from Suriname and
Curacao, both former Dutch colonies. Complaining to friends
in transatlantic phone calls that Black people in the Netherlands
were much too colonized, folks laughed and reminded me of
white Dutch involvement in the imperialist colonization of
South Africa and the institutionalization of white supremacy.
This is a history white Dutch people do not want to acknowledge. Again and again, when I talked with them about the ways
white supremacy asserts itself in Dutch culture, I was told that
I did not understand, that "there is really no racism in the
Netherlands." Yet, when I talked to politically aware Black
folks, I heard the same stories of racial harassment and terrorism that Black Americans tell one another in the States. If we
were sitting in public spaces, these Black folks would talk in
hushed, low voices, fearful of being overheard by white authority figures who want only to hear those Black voices which
insist racism does not exist in Holland.

I was not shocked or surprised at the verdict reached in

241

Why L.A. Happened

Simi Valley. It seemed fully in keeping with the anti-Black backlash that is on the rise in the United States. That backlash was signalled by the global broadcasting of the Clarence Thomas hearings. His appointment to the Supreme Court was a public announcement to all that this country was no longer interested in the issue of racial justice. And it became even clearer when Thomas, as a member of the Court, worked to undermine major civil rights gains.

Realizing that the Simi Valley verdict was predictable, I wondered why Black folks had not worked out a strategic response before the court's decision was announced. Our collective failure to predict the outcome and organize meaningful responses prior to the announcement of the verdict was deeply disturbing. It suggested that Black Americans have collectively ceased to be politically vigilant. On one hand, the achievements of contemporary civil rights movements and Black liberation struggle, racial integration and class mobility, have lulled some of us into believing that racial justice has become a reality, a norm even. Masses of Black people who continue to believe that the legal system will provide a just and fair hearing were genuinely convinced that the evidence of the King video alone would insure that he would win his case. Others of us, particularly the Black underclass, despaired precisely because the gains of contemporary progressive political movements have had so little concrete impact on our lives. To these folks, continued white supremacist oppression and exploitation indicated that progressive struggle for change had not worked. Many of these folks simply believe there is no hope that Black people can politically intervene within the existing structure in ways that will be liberating.

Watching the various expressions of "Black rage" in the wake of the verdict on CNN in the city of Utrecht, I was overwhelmed by sadness. For I felt that the manner of protest I was seeing, solely that which was presented through the eyes of white dominated mass media (images of random violence and looting), were tragic expressions of powerlessness and not strategic confrontations with the white supremacist power structure. This led me into a series of self-interrogations. How had I and other aware Black people failed, since we have clearly not shared in a meaningful way our understanding of strategic confrontation with the masses of Black people? I reflected on the growing gap between politically progressive Black folks who are not underclass and that Black underclass which not only suffers severely from racial harassment and assault but is also often paralyzed by rage that threatens to implode. When it *ex*plodes, as in the case of underclass and poor Black responses to the verdict, it leads to misguided destruction. It was as though we were dropping bombs that landed on our own communities, hurting other Black people, destroying our homes, our jobs and businesses that, however corrupt, existed to serve our needs. Seeing this picture from a distance, realizing that it was distorted and incomplete (I knew there were other more organized protests that mass media was simply not showing), I could not help but feel that the initial expressions of protest signalled a major shift in Black American response to racial injustice.

Many of the Black folks who sat at those segregated counters in Woolworth's and other stores to protest the white supremacist system of apartheid, who refused to take seats on segregated buses during the boycotts were, though poor and underclass, politically sophisticated enough to know that rights would not be gained by burning and looting. The young Black activists of the past were not as deeply seduced by the culture of materialism as Black youth are today. We did not believe that freedom was about material wealth. Today, masses of young Black people, from all classes, believe that freedom is determined solely by the extent to which one will have access to material goods, not even material well-being, but *goods*. It is this loss of a meaningful understanding of freedom and liberation that makes it impossible for many Black people to engage in effective political protest.

If freedom struggle is about fighting to gain access to material goods, then looting is the right strategy. And if the prevailing sentiment is that by destroying goods and property you have attacked white supremacy, then that too can take place with little organization, with no leadership. While it is clear that in the aftermath of the verdict much meaningful political protest has been organized and new strategies for challenging racial injustice implemented, African Americans cannot afford to ignore the truths that come to light when we critically examine the implications of the initial protests.

I was asked again and again by reporters in the Netherlands to explain why Black people thought violence and looting was an effective means of protest. Though many Europeans felt that the Simi Valley verdict indicated the extent to which the United States does not support human rights or live out democratic ideas of racial justice, this indictment did not lead them to interpret the responses of Black people with a sympathetic viewpoint. Black rage at racial injustice is always perceived as misguided, irrespective of the forms that rage takes. Again and again, I informed white reporters that the Black folks who were destroying property and looting were not engaging in some aberrant behavior. That they in fact were showing just how American they are, for material goods and property are what we are socialized to believe really matters, not human life or human well-being. Hence, it is perfectly in keeping with the dominant values of the culture for enraged Black folks to target their aggression at material objects. Would more strategic, politically sophisticated forms of protest have received the global media coverage that was given the violent acts and looting?

Unfortunately, much of the violence and looting deflected attention away from the awesome injustice of the King affair. To some extent, the legal system's betrayal of democratic ideals of peace and justice was replaced by global concern with issues of law and order. And ultimately, many whites (and even conservative Blacks and other peoples of color) felt that despite the blatant brutality and subsequent injustice of the verdict, the more important issue was establishing systems of control that would check the violent impulses of oppressed and exploited; hence, the incident was used to justify and reinforce white supremacy. All over the world, white supremacist governments are concerned with how to control "unruly" Black folks, how to impose law and order so that property and commodities can be kept "safe." If Black folks and our allies in struggle remain committed to eradicating white supremacy, then we must refuse to accept any notion of freedom that makes it synonymous with materiality. Clearly, Black folks must no longer endorse through silence or complicity the idea that freedom is solely about the right to material gain and that random violence and destruction is an acceptable response to injustice. In "Facing the Challenge of A New Age," Martin Luther King calls for "freedom and justice through love," admonishing us to remember:

> There is nothing in all the world greater than freedom. It is worth paying for; it is worth losing a job; it is worth going to jail for. I would rather be a free pauper than a rich slave. I would rather die in abject poverty with my convictions than live in inordinate riches with the lack of self-respect.

One lesson Black folks must learn from the initial protests following the announcement of the verdict is that we must hold steadfast to an idea of freedom that is firmly rooted in the recognition of our subjectivity, of our oppositionality, of our willingness to move beyond the values of the dominant society.

BELL HOOKS is a writer and professor. Her previous books include *Ain't I A Woman, Feminist Theory, Talking Back, Yearning, Breaking Bread* and most recently a book of essays, *Black Looks: Race and*

Why L.A. Happened

Representation (all by South End Press) and the forthcoming book of poems, *the woman's mourning song* (Harlem Rivers Press).

L.A. 1992:

Race, Class and Spiritual Poverty in the American Empire

Bartley L. McSwine

Most great societies have not declined because of their strengths, but because of cultural weaknesses that have led to insurmountable internal contradictions—contradictions which have led to either precipitous decline from within or to such a weakened condition that they have easily been conquered by enemies from without. Edward Gibbon in *The Decline and Fall of the Roman Empire* points to the breakdown in moral and ethical values within that society which led to the eventual deterioration of the State. At an even earlier period in history, ancient Egypt, after several thousand years of history, began to decline after internal contradictions left it vulnerable to invasions first from the Hyksos, then from the Persians and later from the Greeks, the Romans, the Nubians, the Arabs and the Ottoman Turks.

Cheikh Anta Diop, in his *African Origin of Civilization,* states that the Sixth Dynasty in Ancient Egypt was to end with the first popular uprising in that nation's history. He goes on to state that:

> ...division of labor on the basis of craftsmanship already existed. The cities doubtless were active centers of trade

247

with the eastern Mediterranean. Their idle poverty-stricken masses would take an active part in the revolt. The mores of the nobility created a special class of men: servants contracted for varying tenure. The...country had plunged into anarchy; insecurity reigned, especially in the Delta with the raids by "Asiatics." The latter monopolized jobs intended for Egyptians in the various workshops and urban building yards. The wretched of Memphis, capital and sanctuary of royalty, pillaged the city, robbing the rich and driving them into the streets. The movement soon spread to other cities. Sais was temporarily governed by a group of ten notables.

Diop goes on to quote from Jacques Pirenne's *Histoire de la Civilisation de l'Egypte Ancienne*:

Thieves become proprietors and the former rich are robbed. Those dressed in fine garments are beaten. Ladies who had never set foot outside now go out. The children of nobles are dashed against the walls. Towns are abandoned. Doors, walls, columns are set aflame. The offspring of the great are thrown into the street. Noble ladies flee malcontents. Peasants wear shields into the fields. Man slays his own brother. The roads are traps. People lie in ambush until [the farmer] returns in the evening; then they steal whatever he is carrying. Beaten with cudgels, he is shamefully killed. Cattle roam at will; no one attends them...

Each man leads away any animals he has branded...Everywhere crops are rotting; clothing, spices, oil are lacking. Filth covers the earth. The government stores are looted and their guards struck down. People eat grass and drink water. So great is their hunger that they eat the food intended for the swine. The dead are thrown into the river; the Nile is a sepulcher. Public records are no longer secret....

Diop concludes: "So the first cycle of Egyptian history ended with the collapse of the Old Kingdom. It had begun with the feudalism that preceded the first political unification; it closed in anarchy and feudalism."

Alexis De Tocqueville, writing in the 19th century after his visit to this country from France, and still later Gunnar Myrdal, writing after his visit from Sweden, spoke of similar contradictions in America between rich and poor, Black and white. Echoing W.E.B. DuBois who had said in 1906 that the problem of the 20th century was the problem of the color line, Myrdal concluded in 1944 that this problem of race was a major American Dilemma, that if not dealt with would tear this society apart. The promise of white society as reflected in the U.S. Constitution, the Pledge of Allegiance, the Gettysberg Address and the general ethos of equality as promoted by these documents, contrasted sharply with the reality of poverty and prejudice as practiced on a daily basis, he said. The recent uprising in Los Angeles and other major cities across this country are a manifestation of these contradictions in the late 20th century American empire.

New York Senator Bill Bradley has said that the original sin was slavery. And certainly to a large extent this is true insofar as African Americans are concerned. But the Rodney King brutality verdict and the popular uprising that it touched off spoke not of an original sin but of original sins that have never been atoned for, original sins that have been forgotten, ignored and denied by all except those who experienced them.

It would probably be too harsh to describe late 20th century America as a feudal society in the same sense that one would call medieval England or ancient Egypt feudal societies (although they have many of the same characteristics). However, I believe it not inaccurate to say that America is a colonial empire. From the year 1500 to around the turn of this century (1900), the taming of the West resulted in the reduction of the Native American community from a population of 40 million to 75,000—a condition that would normally be referred to as genocide despite the fact that no gas ovens were used. This meant that for Native Americans, more than 90% of their population was destroyed with the remainder being placed on reservations. The explicit purpose of the reservations was to civilize people who were considered savages and heathens. The harsh reality is that their land was taken away and most of them destroyed. Many Americans do not realize this nor do they realize that those reservations are still in existence today.

When Mexican Americans look at their history, they see the land that once belonged to them via Mexico (California, New Mexico, Utah, Colorado, Arizona and Texas) now is a part of the American empire. And even though it is no longer against the law to speak Spanish in public schools in Texas, the fight for bilingual education in Texas and other states is a long way from being settled.

For African Americans, the colonization process is similar and just as devastating. W.E.B. DuBois estimates that from the 16th through the 19th centuries some 15 million slaves were brought to this country—900,000 in the 16th century, 2.75 million in the 17th, 7 million in the 18th and more than 4 million in the 19th. This meant that 12 generations of Blacks experienced the holocaust of slavery—which meant loss of language, culture, identity and the resulting institutionalization of shame connected with who you are and where you came from.

In political terms this means that America, like no other empire that I am aware of, finds itself at the beginning of the 21st century confronted directly with the dilemma that DuBois, Myrdal and others spoke about: how does a nation, built on the exploitation of other people, atone for the crimes of its past without giving up the land it has taken and giving back the souls it has destroyed? If it continues to preach freedom and does not actually provide it for the masses who are homeless, jobless, underemployed, uneducated and without hope, it is only a matter of time before Diop's description of the demise of the Sixth Dynasty in Egypt can be applied here as well.

Race, Class and Spiritual Poverty in the American Empire

Los Angeles 1992 was a poignant warning for the power elite in America. But that warning was also a warning for middle-class Blacks and other Americans as well. For unlike the Watts rebellion of 1965, which was largely confined to the Black community and in which, by and large, only the lower-class Black businesses were destroyed, Los Angeles 1992 was a city-wide, indeed nation-wide, uprising. Not only were Black businesses in South Central Los Angeles destroyed, but all the Korean ones as well. Businesses in Hollywood and Beverly Hills were destroyed. Many middle-class Black businesses, such as the exclusive Golden Bird restaurant and the Aquarian Book Shop, one of the country's oldest Black book stores, were destroyed.

Rebellions also occurred in cities like Las Vegas, Atlanta, San Francisco and Phoenix—primarily precipitated by lower-class Blacks. I say primarily because a large number of Hispanics participated and to a much lesser extent some whites as well. Indeed, there were almost as many Hispanics killed in Los Angeles as Blacks.

In other words, what the nation witnessed in Los Angeles was as much a class rebellion as it was a race rebellion—directed for the most part at the white establishment, but for the first time, not exclusively. The message of Los Angeles is that those without power and privilege are beginning to view anyone that appears to have power and privilege as suspect—as a part of the power structure that institutionalizes a permanent underclass.

When I first arrived in Los Angeles in the early 1960s, Sam Yorty was still mayor and William Parker was the chief of police. Having grown up in a comparatively small city in Texas, I found L.A. a simply fascinating place to live. There was the warmth of the year-round sun, air that by today's standards could be called clean, beaches that drew the ever present sun-worshippers and bathers and nearby mountains reachable by freeways that were really free. By the time I left Los Angeles in the late 1980s, the freeways had become

Why L.A. Happened

clogged arteries of a hemorrhaging city about to have its last stroke. The air had become stagnant, dank and polluted. Freeway shootings had become common, and drive-by shootings were occurring at an epidemic pace. The mayor was now Tom Bradley, a former Black police officer who often bragged while campaigning for office that as a policeman, he never had to pull his gun. Bradley has proven to be a significant improvement over Sam Yorty but, nevertheless, is still trapped like every big city mayor by bureaucratic encapsulation and little money or power to make any real changes in the lives of the poor. Thus, while Bradley has been mayor, homelessness in Los Angeles has grown to an all time high, and unemployment among Black and Latino youth has skyrocketed. Welfare rolls have grown, and in general, the city has deteriorated like all other major cities in this country.

As a youth not long out of high school in the 1960s, however, most of the underside of the city went unnoticed. I was caught up in trying to make it in college and trying to prove to myself and others that a Black boy from racially segregated Texas could make it in the integrated white world of Los Angeles. My awareness of the city's underside was slow in coming, but the thundering force of its wretched misery eventually caught up with my untrained eye; the glitter of the stars along Hollywood Boulevard and the manicured lawns in Beverly Hills could no longer hide the contemptible politics of race and class that continued to use the police as an occupying force in poor and working class communities.

Before Latasha Harlins (a Black teenager whose murder by a Korean shop owner was captured on videotape months before the Rodney King incident) and Rodney King, there was the Leonard Deadwyler case which occurred shortly after I first moved to L.A. Leonard Deadwyler was a Black man who was killed by police while rushing his pregnant wife to the hospital. Apparently having run several traffic lights, the police became suspicious and stopped him. The reports of what happened after that are confusing, but the police claim that when Deadwyler got out of his car, the car lurched forward, and he looked like he was reaching for a gun. No gun was ever found at the scene, and nothing happened to the police involved. Gradually I became aware that the Leonard Deadwyler case was not an isolated incident. I learned of the many Leonard Deadwylers and the police who were always let off with justifiable homicide. There was a definite pattern to these crimes. The victims almost always were Black males shot by white male police officers. I wondered why if I could see this pattern others could not. Then I learned that justice is not color blind but indeed very color conscious.

The *Dallas Times Herald* published a study back in October of 1989 that examined more than 4,000 district attorney case files. It found that for similar crimes, Blacks and Hispanics almost always received longer sentences than whites.

	BLACKS (years)	HISPANICS (years)	WHITES (years)
Aggravated Assault	7.60	7.25	5.29
Murder	35.86	30.43	32.61
Attempted Murder	22.53	14.56	9.36
Rape	26.19	12.89	21.43
Burglary	11.18	8.34	9.67

This pattern held for not only first convictions, but also for second and third convictions as well. And, no doubt, this same pattern holds true not only for Los Angeles, but for all the other major cities in this country.

After living in L.A. for awhile, one discovers that the city is a metaphor for the materialism and superficiality sought by the rest of the country. Everyone is defined by the movie industry which to insiders is known by its euphemism, The Industry. I remember once when my daughter was visiting me from Chicago when she was about nine or ten. The one thing she wanted to do that summer was to visit the Hollywood sign that is seen so often on television overlooking Los Angeles from the Hollywood Hills like a demi-god or patron saint. She wanted to be able to tell her friends when she went back to Chicago that she had actually seen and taken a picture of The Sign. It was not her fault. The industry has affected the whole country in the same way. You might be discovered, become rich and live in Hollywood or Beverly Hills, marry rich, divorce early and spend the rest of your life seeing a shrink. It is no accident that the divorce rate in Los Angeles is one of the highest in the country. Eric Fromm has described this phenomenon as the destruction of love in capitalistic societies. You become a commodity; your body, if it is a perfect ten, has high commodity value; relationships become commoditized; and who you are as an individual becomes lost in the tinsel town materialism you have come to worship. Alas, very few ever measure up to who or what The Industry says you are supposed to be. Thus, it is no accident that the city that creates the greatest psychological, economic and physical distance between people also creates this same distance between the haves and the have nots. Alienation and commoditization become the norm, and spiritual poverty reigns throughout the land.

There were other even more poignant ways in which I began to experience the city as I encountered it on a day-to-day basis. I soon learned that the alienation and commoditization could manifest themselves as violence in any number of ways. When I first arrived in L.A., I was completely unaware of red light districts. Certainly there had been prostitution in Texas, but it was hush hush and undercover. I soon learned that L.A. had many such districts where one could literally see the commodities parading around almost naked. It seemed strange, even surreal, to see women, particularly Black women, walking up and down the streets selling sex.

Then there was my encounter with the Los Angeles Police

Department—the LAPD. I had only a few minor parking violations when one day, not long after my marriage, I was driving down Hollywood Boulevard to a dealership to get my car fixed. I had been driving relatively slowly because of the problem with my car when I noticed a police car behind me. It seemed to be unusually close, but I tried to ignore it because I knew I hadn't done anything wrong. Then I noticed a second police car pull up behind the first one, and immediately a sense of dread came over me. After I made a couple of turns and they were still behind me, I knew something was wrong. By the time I arrived at my destination—the car dealership—a third police car was pulling up from another direction—apparently the reinforcements he had called for. As I pulled into the dealer's lot the siren of the car directly behind me started to wail. An officer was immediately out of his car coming toward me with his hand on his gun. He and now five other officers ordered me to get out of my car, to turn around, place my hands on top of my car and spread eagle my legs. When I asked what was wrong, what had I done, I was abruptly told to shut up.

So there I stood, with my back to these officers, at least one of whom now had his gun drawn, wondering what I had done, wondering whether I would be dead in the next minute. By now, a large crowd had gathered and the absurd, impossible nature of all that was going on bore in on me. Flashes of death continued to enter my mind. "Black man killed while resisting arrest," the headline would say. Arrest! What had I done? Why wouldn't they tell me? But then I knew in the deep recesses of my mind that I didn't have to do anything but be Black. What had all those Black men done who had become strange fruit on southern trees? What had Emmit Till done? What had Sam Hose done—the Black man whose fingers and toes were exhibited in a meat market after he had been hung in Atlanta? Martin Luther King? Malcolm X? The Scottsboro Boys? A scene from Kafka's *The Trial* raced through my mind. What had Joseph "K" done? He was arrested one fine morning and taken to jail without explanation! I later learned that a Black man had stolen a car that was the same color as the one I was driving. I never found out whether it was the same make or model. But there was no doubt in my mind that it was the same color! Needless to say, I was traumatized by the whole incident. I was literally sweating and shaking with fear. And just as quickly as they had come, the squad cars drove away. But the crowd still milled about. I could see in their faces and feel from their glare the lingering wonder of whether I was guilty or not. There was no doubt that I had been convicted by some, or at least that is the way I felt. I slowly drove home without even attempting to get my car fixed. My body was in tack, but the scars this incident left on my mind still remain. So now when I think of violence, I think of this incident doubled many times over; it happens to Blacks not only in L.A. but throughout this country every day.

I have had a strong belief for a while now that Martin Luther King and Malcolm X were killed because they were trying to unite all oppressed people in this country. I still believe that. The forces that unleashed the Tuskegee Experiment, that return Haitians to oppression, that treat the farm workers as feudal serfs, that are more interested in building prisons than public schools, that still maintains and supports a feudal Indian reservation system run by hang-around-the-fort half-breeds—these forces are obviously still very active in this society. And it has become increasingly clear that the sinister level of their operations has become increasingly sophisticated. I define spiritual poverty as the absence of a conscience, the absence of love, the absence of a soul. It is a state of denial so great as to cause hysterical blindness. This is the condition of America today as it enters the 21st century. It is a bill that James Baldwin said must be paid.

DR. BART MCSWINE is an associate professor in the College of

Education at Chicago State University. He has taught at California State University, Paul Quinn College and Tuskegee University. He is also a consultant to public schools and text book publishers in multicultural and African-centered education.

Black Must Be Beautiful Again

Bebe Moore Campbell

What shook Los Angeles on April 29, was not the earthquake I was expecting. I'm an East Coast woman, Philly born and bred. I was raised in a town where the ground, at least, stayed put, and in the eight years that I've spent in my adopted West Coast home, my constant fear has been that the place would be shaken apart by 10 seconds of cataclysmic natural forces while I screamed from inside a stalled elevator. And so I stocked up on bottled water and canned goods and memorized emergency measures: stay calm; check for injuries; clean up dangerous spills—all the while praying that the much feared disaster would leave L.A. in peace for another millennium.

But that city's peace has been irrevocably shattered. In the aftermath of the Rodney King brutality verdict, the trembler that ripped L.A. into screaming fragments was measured, not by a Richter scale, but in blood and flames; the upheaval came, not from the bowels of the earth but from the depths of human anguish and rage. The pain rumbled through hearts as well as the streets.

The Los Angeles rebellion of 1992 is still for now, but the tally of human and material annihilation has broken all previ-

Why L.A. Happened

ous records for American civil unrest: 51 dead; 2,383 injured; more than 600 fires; nearly 15,000 arrests; and at least $785 million in property damage. Watts, Newark and Detroit pale in comparison. The largest urban disturbance in United States history left a landscape strewn with rubble, devastation and trampled dreams. Days, even weeks after the urban unrest that turned neighborhood blocks into smoky ashes, the news shows are still replaying their tapes, as if there is some lesson for us all hidden in the images of ruin. There is a cacophony of cries to rebuild Los Angeles, and surely that must be done. There are neighborhoods with no grocery stores, where women now must board city buses to buy bread, eggs and milk for their families; 4,000 people mourn their lost jobs, and many uninsured merchants are bankrupt, with little hope of ever resurrecting their razed shops without financial intervention. Certainly, there are pressing economic woes that must be addressed.

But if burned and looted businesses demand presidential and national attention, the reconstruction that African Americans must immediately concern ourselves with and ultimately give our full regard to isn't one that will be composed of bricks and mortar, but of hearts and souls. For African Americans, there is an essential truth hidden amidst the ruins: we must love ourselves back to emotional health first, and then economic well being.

As I look at communities that have been scorched by the wrath of an enraged and oppressed people I am reminded of earthquake emergency measures: there is a dangerous spill seeping across the land; most of us are injured, and calm can no longer be guaranteed. And yet, we are all looking for a way to make sense of the devastation, and none of us want to be visited again by either angry hordes bent on destruction or trucks full of armed federal troops. We are seeking hope. But many of us are looking in the wrong direction.

Hope for African Americans is not in government loans or enterprise zones. We cannot put our faith in Peter Ueberroth or President Bush or the Supreme Courts, nor can we hold our breath waiting for justice. Ultimately, we cannot afford to look for either vindication or validation that comes from outside us. We must rebuild our communities, but first we must rebuild our minds. In 1992, as the embers of Los Angeles still smolder, the challenge that African Americans face is the same one we have always faced, only now there is an urgency that we can no longer ignore—we must finally negotiate and translate our slave heritage and the single, cruelest legacy of that 246-year odyssey: the unconscious belief in our inferiority, a mindset that leads to a lack of self-love. We must seek absolute healing not because we are sick, but because we have been wounded by centuries of oppression and denigration, because we are bleeding internally and the injuries we have sustained sap our strength and rob us of our greatness. And yet, the balm that we need isn't mysterious or rare, indeed, it's one we've used before.

Black must become beautiful again, and this time we must mean it.

The slogan has an eerie, nostalgic ring and evokes the ghost of platform shoes, mile high 'fros, bright colored dashikis, raised fists and As Salaam Alaikum. I say those words, and I am young again, swaying to the strains of Marvin Gaye. For those of us who lived through that time, the era is memorable not because of its style, but because of the sweet promises it rendered. Arguably, no period has ever been as empowering, as self-affirming for African Americans. The '60s was when, collectively, we began to move toward loving ourselves. We began to embrace our hair, our color, our features and doing so made us stronger. The trouble is, that brief shining moment of self-love didn't last long enough. Didn't go deep enough. The '60s gave us the prescription for healing, but we failed to take the strong medicine necessary for the cure.

We had things to do other than attend to the pain deep inside of us. We were marching, sitting in, lying in, trying to integrate. And the fact that we succeeded in sitting next to white people, in going to their schools, eating at their restaurants and working next to them convinced some of us that we were as good as they were. That being with white people was all the healing that was needed. We didn't have to attend to the feelings inside of us, the ones that quietly and persistently said that no, we weren't good at all. We said Black is beautiful, but we didn't believe it.

The fires of 1992 call for a new movement, a revolution of the spirit. The demonstrations we hold now must be personal and emotional. The marches we attend must be in our minds. We must campaign for self-love and healing as though our very lives are at stake. They are.

African Americans should address the challenge of loving ourselves with the courage of Rosa, Martin, Malcolm and Fannie Lou, rolling up our sleeves to do the hard emotional work within our families, with our neighbors and friends, in our churches and while we're waiting in barbershops and at the beauty parlor. This is the time to challenge the taboos and start talking out our ancient pain. We have to tell each other our stories, the ones that make us scream: the stories about being the darkest or the lightest in the family; the tales about being passed over for promotions; the ones about growing up on welfare and still feeling ashamed because some in our family remain financially dependent on the government. The stories about hating the width of our noses, the darkness of our eyes, the kink of our hair. About being scared of white folks. Still. Of feeling *less than*. Even now. Let's talk about the pain that imprisons us, and then let's read the books, say the affirmations and prayers, do the mental exercises, form the support groups, and yes, communicate with the therapists who will help us break out of our emotional jails. We can learn to love and value ourselves. The '90s is a good time to take up the journey where we left off. We are immersed in a decade where self-awareness and self-help have become the mantras of the masses, where 12-step programs have freed people of addictions. African Americans can benefit from the new knowledge, and we can mine our own psychological experts for specific techniques to address our emotional distress. By any means necessary. We must do whatever must be done to heal ourselves. Black must become beautiful again, and this time, we must mean it.

Self-love and prosperity are inextricably linked. When we love ourselves, we'll buy what we can afford instead of what we think we need to affirm us, and we'll save the difference for a business in our own neighborhood. When we love ourselves fully, recycling Black dollars won't be an option; it will be an obsession. Loving ourselves means we won't go to Beverly Hills or Fifth Avenue to shop until we have exhausted all the Black-owned possibilities in our own communities. At last we will recognize that the white man's ice isn't colder, just more expensive.

Self-love and motivated children are inextricably linked. When we love ourselves, we can find the time to help those who look like us, whether this means adopting a class as a group, becoming a big sister or brother, tutoring, or encouraging Black children whenever we can. When we love ourselves, we get involved with Black children who are at risk, not because it's our duty, but because they are our children, and not helping them is not only unimaginable, it is obscene.

Racism will never disappear. America will never be fair to all of its people. African Americans can learn to respond to racial discrimination in a self-affirming and not a self-defeating way. The healing of Los Angeles begins with each one of us. And no, this revolution isn't going to be televised; its going to be internalized. When we finally stop asking America to love us and begin to love ourselves, we will prosper as a people. Our giant step forward will cause the ground beneath our feet to tremble as no earthquake ever has; we will believe in our dreams, and that alone will make them come true.

Up, ye mighty race, you can accomplish what you will. Say it loud: I'm Black, and I'm proud. Salaam Alaikum, sisters and brothers. Black must be beautiful again. And this time we must mean it.

BEBE MOORE CAMPBELL is the author of *Your Blues Aint Like Mine, Sweet Summer: Growing Up With and Without Dad* and *Successful Women and Angry Men.* She is a regular commentator on National Public Radio and her articles have appeared in the *New York Times* and the *Washington Post.*

Heat Wave

Joyce Ann Joyce

Approximately two weeks after the fires began to cool in South Central Los Angeles, I wandered into a video store, looking for something to distract me from the disappointment and pain I was feeling because of the loss of real political leadership in this so-called greatest country on the planet. Because it was a Friday afternoon, all of the newly released tapes had been rented: *The Fisher King, Robin Hood, Frankie and Johnny, The Super* and all the *Lethal Weapons.* So I sauntered around the store and ended up in the drama section of old tapes. Black faces on one tape stood out. And because those faces included James Earl Jones and Cicely Tyson, I decided that they would keep me well enough entertained.

Once I got the tape home and put it in the VCR, I remembered that I already had seen this movie on television. I realized that if the Elders were correct (as they usually are), some good reason (that was not clear to me at the time) was responsible for my stumbling upon the movie *Heat Wave*, recorded by Turner Entertainment and based on the true story of Robert Richardson's account of the Watts riots in 1965. The movie (or Richardson's account) did not provide me with the solace that I was seeking when I entered the video store.

Why L.A. Happened

Providing the answers to the many questions that I have heard posed since the Simi Valley jury returned its 'not guilty' verdict, *Heat Wave* demonstrates quite effectively and poignantly the causes of both the Watts riots in August 13, 1965 and of the most recent Los Angeles riot following the jury's decision.

Even though I myself find it quite a conundrum that I currently live in Nebraska, I have always wondered why and how so many Blacks ended up in California, a state quite a distance from those southern states which were the breeding places of millions of children of slaves. *Heat Wave* not only answers this question, but it also makes it quite clear that the white mentality in California was as hostile toward Blacks as it was in the South from which the Blacks had fled.

Thinking that California was the real land of opportunity, Clifford Turbin, his wife, son J. T and a cousin slightly older than their son, Richard Robertson, sing and clap their hands along the road as they discuss happily the good schools and the airplane and aluminum factories that will provide them with a livelihood quite different from that in Alabama. They tease each other and discuss with pride those Black movie stars, like Leona Horne and Dorothy Dandridge, whom they see as having crossed racial boundaries.

As they drive into the community where Clifford's mother-in-law (Ma Dear) lives, the wholesomeness of this Black California neighborhood contrasts sharply to the shanties and poverty of Black Alabama in the 1950s displayed at the very beginning of the movie. Of course, the street on which Ma Dear (Cicely Tyson) lives is in Watts. Thus, though her house is comfortable and nicely furnished, it soon becomes clear to Clifford and his family that Alabama's rural squalor and racism is even more vicious and debilitating in sunny California.

At dinner, Ma Dear cautions J.T. and Bobby (Richardson) against going on Alameda Street. Since the two young men think that California is nothing like Alabama, they pay no attention to the warning nor to where they are when they end up lost on Alameda street searching for Hollywood. Suddenly, these two young men find themselves in a dilemma quite characteristic of their life in Alabama. A car full of young white ruffians (easily recognized as rednecks in Alabama) chase J.T. and Bobby for a short while in the car. When the car proves ineffective, they get out of the car and run after the two Black men until they escape across a railroad track just in front of a passing train. After the train passes and the Blacks are safe outside the forbidden territory, one of the young whites screams, "Niggers, stay out of Linwood."

This incident proves to be merely an introduction to what follows. The spirit with which Clifford Turbin and his family sang "If you traveling on the road tell him what you want" as they crossed the California state line slowly fades as they struggle to make a new life. While Clifford first experiences California's unwritten Jim Crow laws as he struggles for employment, his son J.T. faces what racism has done to the mentality of middle-class Blacks who have adopted the Booker T. Washington strategy. In suit, tie, suspenders and a cheerful smile, Clifford goes from one construction site to another for weeks looking for employment, only to be told that either the position has been filled or the company is looking for someone with more experience. This proud, capable Black man who had been a construction foreman with 45 men working under him in the South has to take a job as a janitor in order to provide, even to a small degree, for his family.

Facing similar obstacles, J.T. goes excitedly into the counselor's office at school to explain that he wants to be a pilot like his great uncle who was one of the Tuskegee pilots. The counselor discourages him by saying that a knowledge of navigation and hydraulics is required for which calculus and physics are prerequisites. J.T. explains that he made a B- in chemistry before coming West and that he even tutored some of the other students in his school. The counselor continues her attack of his spirit by saying that J.T.'s college board scores are quite low. The look on J.T.'s face acknowledges that he finally understands the kind of Black person he is talking to. After saying he is not stupid, he walks out of the room. When he meets Bobby (Richardson) who is waiting for him outside, J.T. says he told the woman he wanted to go into auto mechanics. When Bobby asks J.T. what the counselor said, J.T. responds, "Nothing I don't already know." What J.T. knows is the same thing that Richard Wright's Bigger Thomas knows: that being a pilot and being able to fulfill one's potential to its fullest is not an activity allowed a Black man in America. Even many Black people, such as the school counselor, believe that Black men should not aim too high. Thus, Clifford's and his son's dreams are destroyed, and they become victims of alcohol. Their spirits broken, they become aloof and full of self-hatred.

When Bobby returns from the army, he barely recognizes his cousins. Clifford boasts and talks incessantly in the neighborhood barber shop owned by Junius Jackson (James Earl Jones), and he is unable to keep a job as janitor because of his drinking. J.T. is bitter and hostile toward Bobby who is excited about his new job at the *Los Angeles Times*. Bobby, however, is not used as a reporter. He is a message "boy" in a suit. While he is struggling to gain his supervisor's recognition, he and the rest of Watts are constantly harassed by policemen. Clifford and his wife are pulled over; the police throw Clifford against the car and push his wife's purse in her stomach after searching it. Bobby and his girlfriend are stopped because they are walking down the street. When one of the policemen refers to Bobby's girlfriend as "Tricksy Trim," Bobby and she turn and walk away as this same policeman aims a gun at them and orders them to stop. If a new, more sensible and sensitive policeman had not caught up with Bobby and talked to him, the other policeman would have fired without any provocation whatsoever.

The incident from which the Black community was unable to recover began in the same way as the now historical

Rodney King beating. On August 13, 1965, a policeman pulled over two young Black brothers and said that they were speeding. When the policeman detected alcohol on the driver's breath, he asked him to step out of the car. After a crowd gathered, including the driver's mother, he became outraged and said that he would rather die than go to jail. At this point, policemen flooded the Watts neighborhood. Outraged that one Black man was being manhandled by a throng of policemen, the community became angry. One policeman, mistakenly thinking that a pregnant woman spat on his neck, grabbed her and threw her up against the car and into it. By the time the police left with the two brothers and the pregnant woman in custody, the Watts community was uncontrollable. Centuries of racism, powerlessness and disappointment were unleashed in looting and rioting.

News media all over the country compared the pictures of Watts burning in 1965 with the recent fires in South Central L.A. These same media, particularly CNN and Dan Rather, have aired stories about the brave and talented children who live in South Central L.A. They have shown pictures of the young Black men arrested for beating the truck driver. They have even interviewed the mothers of some of these young men. But where are the stories behind what made these young men react as they did? Where are the stories that make it clear that J.T.'s children and Clifford's grandchildren have inherited their father's and grandfather's powerlessness, hopelessness, bitterness and self-hatred?

What happened to Rodney King and the jury's verdict clearly responds to those white liberals and Black accommodationists who have a need to believe that class threatens the Black man in this country more than racism. Neither the Black community nor the white one has profited from history. When the trial was changed from L.A. to Simi Valley, Black leaders all over the country should have been protesting and leading demonstrations. If we had learned

Why L.A. Happened

anything from the Watts riots, the Black community would never have allowed the site of the trial to be changed to the Simi Valley police stronghold. The brick we had at the pit of our stomachs after the verdict should have been hurled at the criminal justice system long before the trial began.

The fact that police brutality provided the ember that ignited the frustrations, anger, bitterness and stifled violence in 1965 and 1992 symbolizes the life of a people whose lives are still governed by the whims of overseers and pattyrollers hired to keep the underclass from forgetting their limitations. Ma Dear expresses these feelings best when she talks to the wealthy white Beverly Hills lawyer for whom she works and who has just brought a gun to shoot the "beast" when they come into his neighborhood. She asks him how he would feel if everything he had ever dreamed had always been close enough to see but never close enough to touch.

None of us are wise enough to know why one sibling from an improvised family survives the horrors and limitations of that environment and becomes a doctor, lawyer, professor or journalist while another from the same home ends up an alcoholic or in prison. What we do know is that like J.T., many alcoholics, who should be airline pilots and who deserve the right to fulfill their dreams, roam the streets. The Watts riots ironically provided Bobby Richardson the opportunity to fulfill his dream. Because whites are beaten up in Watts, Bobby's supervisor is desperate for someone to go into Watts to report the news back to the paper. Bobby aggressively explains that he had saved the lives of two white reporters and that he was the only one at the *L.A. Times* qualified to go into Watts. Though the paper had never used a Black reporter before, the supervisor very reluctantly gives Bobby a reporter's badge. The first story that he telephones in is so good that the paper runs it without any changes.

In the end, a police chief refers to the Black community as monkeys in a zoo; the news media is castigated for looking the other way, and the mayor, who attended a $100 a plate dinner an hour before troops arrived in Watts, is condemned.

Almost thirty years later, L.A. still has a police chief who sees Blacks as monkeys. The news media, federal government and their parent corporations continue to look away from urban development. Black mayors now give the orders to drop bombs on women and children.

In 1966, the *L.A. Times* was awarded the Pulizer Prize for Robert Richardson's coverage of the riots. Even after such a prestigious award, after the forming of a commission to study the riots and after a movie starring some of our finest and most committed Black actors and actresses—and after 27 years of so-called Black progress—more of South Central L.A. is in shambles today than it was in 1965. The actions we take today as Black people must go beyond newspaper stories, beyond the forming of commissions to study problems with causes even our children understand and beyond movies that get lost in the stacks if we are to prevent J.T.'s grandchildren and Clifford's great grandchildren from leading gangs that will destroy their lives and those of many others in the year 2019, 27 years from now. We have all the information we need as well as the brilliant young Black minds and energy to run our own airline and construction companies. What is missing is the means by which we can use this information to become leaders rather than followers in the decades to come.

JOYCE ANN JOYCE is a professor of English and is Associate Director of the Gwendolyn Brooks Literary Center at Chicago State University. She is the author of *Richard Wright's Art of Tragedy* and co-editor of *The New Cavalcade: African American Writing From 1760 to the Present.*

part seven . . .

MORE TO REMEMBER

Bloods/Crips Proposal for LA's Face-Lift

Black-on-Black, Black-on-Brown, Brown-on-Black, Brown-on-Brown—the violence in L.A. is a many-hued tragedy which has led to the deliberate decimation of the area's young male population. For years, the colored warrior men have been swirling like sand tornadoes in a desert storm—fighting, killing, maiming. Then, Black man Rodney King was seen across the world being savagely beaten by the white LAPDs, and the Bloods and the Crips stopped shooting long enough to ask the very poignant question: Who's our real enemy here in L.A.?

One Black man's tragedy was the catalyst for a good historical turnabout to emerge from this sorry affair: the Black men and Brown men of the Bloods and Crips gangs laid down their weapons of war and called a truce. Together they created the following (untouched, unedited) list of demands for cash and opportunities to restore South Central.

To this day (September 1992), despite alleged instigations and underminings of the peace accord by the LAPD, the truce has held firm. **Ed.**

Burned and Abandoned Structures

Every burned and abandoned structure shall be gutted. The city will purchase the property if not already owned by the city, and build a community center. If the structure is on a corner lot or is a vacant lot, the city will build a career

274

counseling center or a recreation area, respectively.

Repavement

All pavements/sidewalks in Los Angeles are in dire need of resurfacing. The Department of Transportation shall pay special attention to the pedestrian walkways and surface streets located in predominantly poor and minority areas. Our organization will assist the city in the identification of all areas of concern.

Lighting

All lighting will be increased in all neighborhoods. Additionally, lighting of city streets, neighborhood blocks and alleyways will be amended. We want a well-lit neighborhood. All alleys shall be painted white or yellow by the building owners and alley lights will be installed at the cost of the owner.

Landscaping

All trees will be properly trimmed and maintained. We want all weeded/shrubbed areas to be cleaned up and properly nurtured. New trees will be planted to increase the beauty of our neighborhoods.

Sanitation

A special task force shall be assigned to focus on the clean-up of all vacant lots and trashed areas throughout the deprived areas. Proper pest control methods shall be implemented by the city to reduce the chances of rodent scattering. The city will declare a neighborhood clean-up week wherein all residents will be responsible for their block—a block captain will be assigned to ensure cooperation. Residents will clean up the block in unisys.

$2 billion shall be appropriated for this effort over and

above existing appropriations.

BLOODS/CRIPS ECONOMIC
DEVELOPMENT PROPOSAL

Loans shall be made available by the federal and state governments to provide interested minority entrepreneurs interested in doing business in these deprived areas. The loan requirements shall not be so stringent that it will make it impossible for a businessman to acquire these loans. These loans shall not exceed a 4% interest bearing charge per year. The businessman shall not be required to have security for the loan, however, the businessman must present at least two years of business operation and taxes, with a city license before funds will be allocated. The owner, must have either an established business desiring to expand or a sound business plan. Assistance for business plans shall be made available to these businessmen by the Small Business Administration. Additionally, the Small Business Administration will provide agents to help each business to develop a sound business plan from beginning to end. No one will be neglected in receiving adequate assistance. These business owners shall be required to hire 90% of their personnel from within their community and the monies shall not be distributed in a lump sum. Funds will be released in increments outlined by the business plan. Any businessman that doesn't conform to the hiring practices will have funding ceased until they conform.

$20 million shall be appropriated for this program over and above existing appropriations.

Please note all grants for these major reconstructions shall be granted to minority-owned businesses. While these minority-owned businesses are doing the work in our communities, they must hire at least 50% of their work force from within the community. NO front organizations will be tolerated!

BLOODS/CRIPS HUMAN WELFARE PROPOSAL

Hospitals and Health Care Centers

Federal government shall provide the deprived areas with three new hospitals and 40 additional health care centers. Dental clinics shall be made available within ten miles of each community. The services shall be free and supported by federal and state funds.

Welfare

We demand that welfare be completely removed from our community and these welfare programs be replaced by state work and product manufacturing plants that provide the city with certain supplies. State monies shall only be provided for individuals and the elderly. The State of California shall provide a child welfare building to serve as day care centers for single parents. We would like to encourage all manufacturing companies to vigorously hire these low income recipients and the state and federal governments shall commit to expand their institutions to provide work for these former welfare recipients.

Parks & Recreation

Los Angeles parks shall receive a complete face-lift, and develop activities and programs in the parks throughout the night. Stages, pools and courts shall be reconstructed and resurfaced, and the city shall provide highly visible security 24 hours a day for these parks and recreational centers. Programs at the park shall be in accordance with educational programs and social exchange programs developed by the city for adults and young adults.

Why L.A. Happened

$1 billion dollars shall be appropriated for this program over and above existing appropriations.

BLOODS/CRIPS EDUCATIONAL PROPOSAL

1. Maximizing education standards in the low income areas is essential to reduce the possibilities of repeated insurrection. The Bloods/Crips propose that:

    a. $300 million will go into the reconstruction and refurbishment of the Los Angeles Unified School District (LAUSD) structures,

    b. $200 million will be donated for computers, supplies and updated books (each student shall have the necessary books),

    c. All teachers' salaries shall be <u>no</u> less than $30,000.00 a year to give them an incentive to educate in our districts, and

    d. Re-election shall be held for all Los Angeles Board of Education members.

2. Reconstruction shall include repainting, sandblasting and reconstruction of all LAUSD schools: remodeling of classrooms, repainting of hallways and meeting areas; all schools shall have new landscaping and more plants and trees around the schools; completely upgrade the bathrooms, making them more modern: provide a bathroom monitor to each bathroom which will provide freshen-up toiletries at a minimum cost to the students (the selling of toiletries will support the salary of the bathroom monitor).

3. A provision for accelerated educational learning programs shall be implemented for the entire LAUSD to provide aggressive teaching methods and provide a curriculum similar to non-economically deprived areas. Tu-

toring for all subjects will be made available to all students after normal school hours. It will be mandatory for all students with sub-level grades to participate.

In these after-school tutorial programs, those students whose grades are up to par will receive federally funded bonus bonds which will be applied to their continued education upon graduation from high school. They will also receive bonus bonds for extra scholastic work towards assisting their fellow students. All institutions shall maintain a second shift of substitute teachers in the schools to enforce educational excellence.

Special financial bonuses shall be given to students who focus on education beyond the school's requirement in the areas of applied math and sciences. High achievers in these areas shall be granted a free trip to another country for educational exchange. Fifty students from each school will be granted this opportunity each year for an indefinite period.

4.   The LAUSD will provide up-to-date books to the neglected areas and enough books to ensure that no student has to share a book with another. Supplies shall be made plentiful and school-sponsored financial programs shall be instituted in order to maintain equipment and supplies for the institution after the first donation.

5.   LAUSD will remove all teachers not planning to further their education along with teachers who have not proven to have a passionate concern for the students in which they serve. All teachers shall be given a standard competency test to verify they are up-to-date with subjects and modern teaching methods. Psychological testing will also be required for all teachers and educational administrators,

including the Los Angeles School Board, every four years.

6.   All curriculums shall focus on the basics in high school requirements and it shall be inundated with advanced sciences and additional applied math, English and writing skills.

7.   Bussing shall become non-existent in our communities if all of the above demands are met.

$700 million shall be appropriated for these programs over and above existing appropriations.

BLOODS/CRIPS LAW ENFORCEMENT PROGRAM

The Los Angeles communities are demanding that they are policed and patrolled by individuals whom live in the community and the commanding officers be ten-year residents of the community in which they serve. Former gang members shall be given a chance to be patrol buddies in assisting in the protection of the neighborhood. These former gang members will be required to go through police training and must comply to all of the laws instituted by our established authorities. Uniforms will be issued to each and every member of the "buddy system," however, no weapons will be issued. All patrol units must have a buddy patrol notified and present in the event of a police matter. Each buddy patrol will be supplied with a video camera and will tape each event and the officers handling the police matter. The buddy patrol will not interfere with any police matter unless instructed by a commanding officer. Each buddy patrol will also be supplied with a vehicle.

$6 million shall be appropriated for this program over and above existing appropriations.

IN RETURN FOR THESE DEMANDS THE BLOODS/CRIPS
ORGANIZATION WILL:

1.   Request the drug lords of Los Angeles take their monies
     and invest them in business and property in Los Angeles.

2.   Encourage these drug lords to stop the drug traffic and get
     them to use the money constructively. We will match the
     funds of the state government appropriations and build
     building-for-building.

3.   Additionally, we will match funds for an aids research and
     awareness center in South Central and Long Beach that
     will only hire minority researchers and physicians to assist
     in the aids epidemic.

CONCLUSION

*Meet these demands and the targeting of police officers
will stop!!*

You have 72 hours for a response and a commitment, in
writing, to support these demands. Additionally, you have 30
days to begin implementation. And, finally, you have four
years to complete the projects of construction of the major
hospitals and restorations.

GIVE US THE HAMMER AND THE NAILS, WE
WILL REBUILD THE CITY.

Why L.A. Happened

BUDGET DEMANDS*

Proposal for LA's Face-Lift	$2,000,000,000
Educational Proposal	700,000,000
Law Enforcement Program	6,000,000
Economic Development Proposal	20,000,000
Human Welfare Proposal	1,000,000,000
TOTAL	**$3,726,000,000**

*To be appropriated over and above existing appropriations.

And in the *Mean* Time:
Final Words

Where is the heart, where is the pulse of hope that our children can attach themselves to? Where are the sources of love that the young innocent can respond to without fear of psychic and physical molestation? What kind of government continues to talk/boast about its richness when its children are the poorest and most deprived? Welcome to family values and Murphy Brown; welcome to one's Vietnam draft status as a major topic for potential presidents; welcome to a political process that disrespects critical thinking; welcome to prime time where 42% of the young Black men (18-35) in the nation's capital are, "enmeshed in the criminal justice system on any given day."* This is the America of L.A., 1992.

Add to all this the unending assault on Blacks worldwide. Two thousand deaths of starvation a day (9/2/92) in Somalia because men with guns do not view their children as priority; hundreds of Haitians perish in the high seas because little

---

*Jason DeParle, *New York Times*, front page, April 18, 1992.

Why L.A. Happened

negroes play at governing on the backs of the poorest; hundreds of Blacks killed in South Africa weekly because white supremacy negates Black life. Do we measure our lives by the misery inflicted upon us? For too many, that is the *only* measurement of life.

MEAN TIME

Going to the gut, without the niceties of language that confuse meanness for meaning, *we are at war*. American prisons hold 750,000 Black men between the ages of 18 and 39—the warrior years. Young Black men are being removed from the streets of the United States like sand in a wind storm. Most of these young brothers never had a chance, never had the guidance, support or inspiration to reach for their dreams—indeed, if they ever learned to dream. Most were nurtured in the culture of denial, poverty and survival. To think beyond next week or next month would be progressive; living for the moment on the fastest streets is the norm.

These are the facts: white men run most of the world, not with small talk or smiles but with force and handouts. This rulership may indeed be dying, but it is not dead yet, nor is it selling any wolf tickets. We must remember that the African Holocaust is not a part of the historical memory of most Blacks, primarily because the winners cover the graves with their cities and golf courses. The winners also write, record and video their history—that's why Columbus (two new films in '92) is so integral to their worldview. African people did not walk on water or fly first class TWA to get here. Men from Europe raped Africa of its people and literally scattered them around the world. In the Western hemisphere there are more than 60 million people of African decent in Brazil speaking Portuguese. There are more than 35 million people of African decent in the U.S. attempting to speak English. Clearly, Black people in the West are not talking to each other. Numbers represent power. But, separated and non-communicative numbers represent ignorance and/or confusion. Most definitely, powerlessness.

These are the facts: (1) In the U.S., white men (the rulership) do not fear white women collectively; individually they have a problem. However, white men and white women are partners, be it senior or junior partners. White women—a significant number—are dissatisfied with their status. That is why there is a strong white women's feminist movement. But in the final analysis, if white people are to replicate, whites must mate with whites. (2) White men do not fear Black women or women of color collectively. Individually, they have all kinds of difficulties with them. However, it is clear that the complexity of colors that exists among Black people is directly attributed to white men raping Black women here and abroad. In fact, there is a saying in South Africa that the colored race did not exist until nine months after white men arrived. (3) White men *fear* Black men collectively and individually. This fear is not spoken of publicly nor debated in the media at all. The core of this fear is not from guilt of past deeds against Blacks but from the uncertainty over how Black men would treat them if ever they gained significant power in the world. They fear that Black men would treat them as they have treated Black men, which has been to unleash untold suffering and death upon them. This fear has little basis in fact or research, it is solely based upon white men's past and present deathdealing actions against the Black race, and Black men in particular.

Values and that which is valuable. Willie Horton elected George Bush. Pat Buchanan sends out an unmistakable message to white America to "take back *our* cities and take back *our* culture and take back *our* country." Guess who *our* is. Values and that which is valuable. During the 1980s, violent crimes increased more than 25%; there were 430 violent crimes per 100,000 according to the Federal Bureau of Investigation. The FBI report also states that "1,429 of every 100,000 black youth were arrested for violent crime in 1990, a rate five times that for white youth." Somehow the rulership would like to forget that poverty stimulates self-protective reactions; poverty in the midst of socially determined riches often fosters violent actions against the *haves* by the *have nots*.

It is common knowledge that America is in serious debt. At the end of 1981, the country owed about $1 trillion; by the end of 1992, the federal debt will be approximately $4 trillion and growing with $290 billion in estimated interest. To most people, these numbers are incomprehensible. They have little meaning to the homeless, the sick without health care, the uneducated, the mothers and fathers fighting to keep their families together. The reality of America is that too many people in the rulership have been lying to us as they confuse and minimize the economic problems. Rather than deal with that issue, the rulership will always play the race card. The tactic is to blame or make a negative case against Blacks and Latinos, and common sense for most whites flies out the door. For most of us who do not make major economic policy decisions for the country, our brains have been mismanaged by the federal and local governments, the media, the church, the educational systems and *Terminator 2*.

As I end this piece, a college officer of the State University of New York at Oneonta released a list of the 125 Black men who are students there to the state police. The state troopers requested the names because of a local crime supposedly committed by a Black man. The ethical/legal implications of his actions came into question only after the students discovered this invasion of their privacy. The logic goes like this: a Black man is accused of committing a crime, therefore, all Black men in the area are suspect. White men are forever committing crimes worldover. Who is drawing up that list? The playing field has never been equal here and never will be.

These are hard words, but I refuse to lie to my children. Racism is a growth industry, especially in an economic depression. From the nations of the former USSR, from Germany to

England, from South Dakota to South Africa, from Atlanta to L.A., real criminals are involved in ethnic cleansing and reworking the political and economic map. Compared to the destruction that may come in America, L.A. and hurricane Andrew will be viewed as a little fire and a big wind.

There is a saying in the Black community: what goes around comes around.

Haki R. Madhubuti

RELATED TITLES PUBLISHED BY
THIRD WORLD PRESS

The Isis Papers: The Keys to the Colors
Dr. Frances Cress Welsing   paper–$14.95   cloth–$29.95

*The Destruction of Black Civilization: Great Issues of a
Race From 4500 B.C. to 2000 A.D.*
Dr. Chancellor Williams   paper–$16.95   cloth–$29.95

*Black Men: Obsolete, Single, Dangerous?: The Afrikan
American Family in Transition*
Haki R. Madhubuti   paper–$14.95   cloth–$29.95

Enemies: The Clash of the Races
Haki R. Madhubuti $12.95

*Nightmare Overhanging Darkly: Essays on Black Culture
and Resistance*
Dr. Acklyn Lynch $14.95

*Chosen People from the Caucasus: Jewish Origins, Delu-
sions, Deceptions and Historical Role in the Slave Trade,
Genocide and Cultural Colonization*
Michael Bradley   cloth–$23.95

*Harvesting New Generations: The Positive Development of
Black Youth*
Useni E. Perkins $12.95

Explosion of Chicago's Black Street Gangs: 1900 to Present
Useni E. Perkins $6.95

Focusing: Black Male-Female Relationships
Dr. Delores P. Aldridge $7.95

The Psychopathic Racial Personality and Other Essays
Dr. Bobby E. Wright $5.95

The Black Anglo-Saxons
Dr. Nathan Hare $12.95

Blacks
Gwendolyn Brooks   paper–$19.95   cloth–$36.95